PRINCIPLES FOR BUILDING IN THE KINGDOM

TONY AZONUCHE

PRINCIPLES FOR BUILDING IN THE KINGDOM

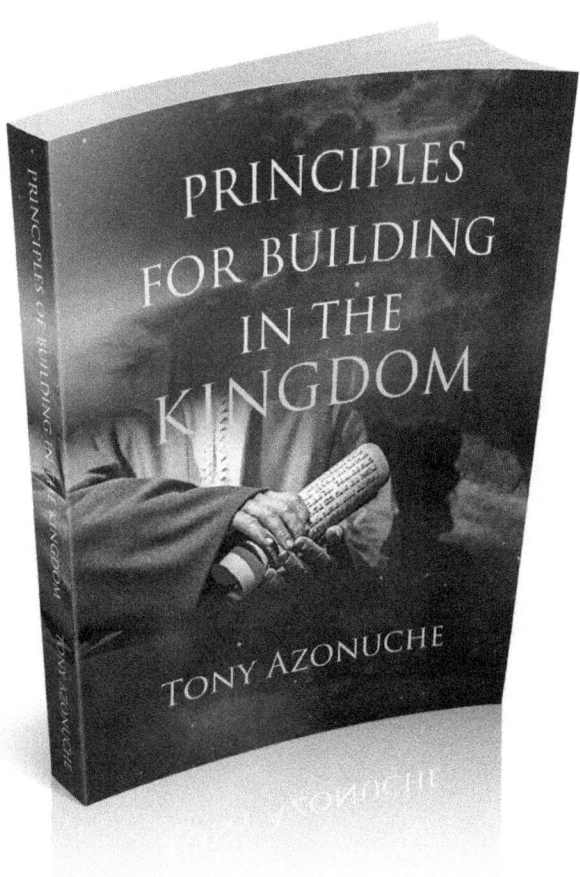

PRINCIPLES FOR BUILDING IN THE KINGDOM

Copyright © 2021 By Tony Azonuche

ISBN: 978-1-64301-027-4

Published in the United States of America by Rehoboth House.

The opinions expressed by the author in this book are exclusively his and not those of Rehoboth House.

All Rights Reserved.
Reproduction of this material, in whole or part, by whatever means, without the express written consent by the author is not permitted.

Unless otherwise indicated, all scripture quotations are taken from the Authorized King James Version of the Holy Bible (KJV).

Contact The Author
Tony Azonuche
tonyazonuche@gmail.com
Tel: 1 (832) 419-7961, (832) 419-7988
Convener: Joshua Generation Movement.
Email: joshuagenmovt@gmail.com
For Teachings, Seminars, Workshops on Kingdom Dimensions

Cover And Interior Designed By Rehoboth House, Chicago
rehobothhouseonline.com
rehobothpublishing@gmail.com
info@rehobothhouseonline.com

Printed In United States Of America, December, 2021

REHOBOTH HOUSE

CONTENTS

Dedication..*ix*

Acknowledgment..*xi*

Endorsement..*xv*

Introduction...*xvii*

Chapter 1: Building In The Accurate Way..1

Chapter 2: Building Principle One: Vision..21

Chapter 3: Building Principle Two: Persuasion.....................................41

Chapter 4: Building Principle Three: Embrace.....................................61

Chapter 5: *Building Principle Four: Confession*....................................77

Chapter 6: *Hindrance To This Building*...95

Chapter 7: *An Awakening To Build*...105

PRINCIPLES FOR BUILDING IN THE KINGDOM

PRINCIPLES FOR BUILDING IN THE KINGDOM

Dedication

I dedicate this work to the almighty God, the possessor of the ends of the earth who alone created us and brought us here on earth for His good pleasure.

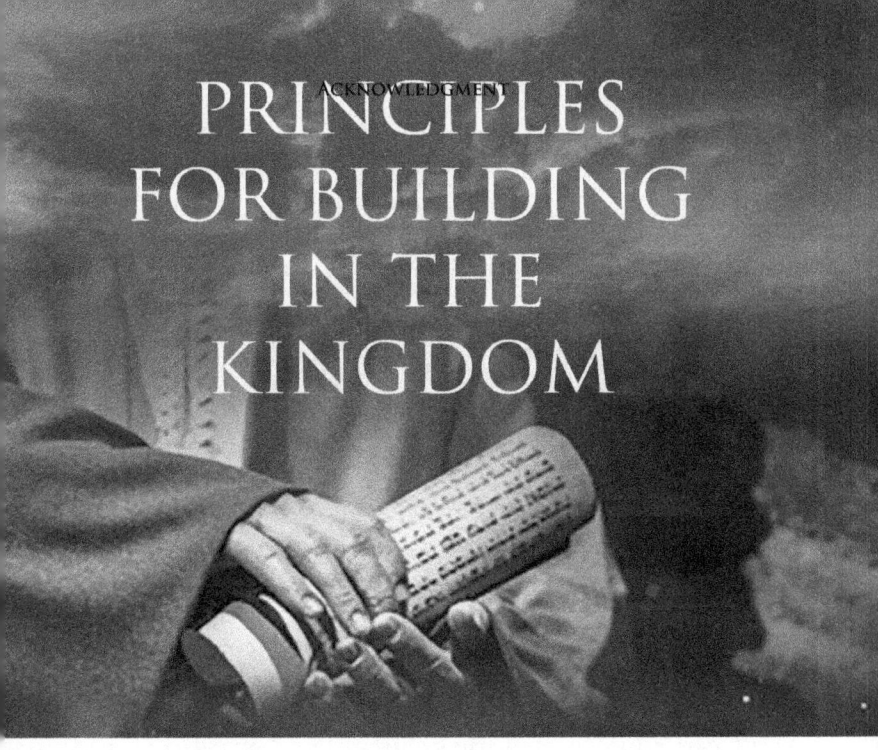

PRINCIPLES FOR BUILDING IN THE KINGDOM

Acknowledgment

This book is entirely a product of divine revelation from the Lord. He gave the idea, so I am here to especially thank Him for the successful production of this piece that has been in my heart for many years. May His name be praised forever and ever. He indeed is the builder of all things. All we do is follow His direction.

I want to appreciate my biological parents Mr. & Mrs. Cyril Azonuche, who brought me into this world and nurtured me to become somebody in life. God wouldn't have used me to produce this work if I had been aborted. Though both are deceased now, I am eternally grateful to them. My shout-out goes to my siblings, whom God used to continue the work my parents couldn't do because of ill-health. You all will not lose your rewards in Jesus' name. Much appreciation goes to my lovely wife and companion for life, Mrs. Favor Obiageli Azonuche. She made obeying God and writing this book easy for me by her understanding and collaboration even at difficult times. The Lord equally gave me beautiful and amazing children: Wisdom, Davida, Deborah, and Joshua. They never gave me trouble that could take me out of tune with God in getting the needed revelation for this book. I love you all.

Great appreciation goes to all the people the Lord used on my way to the journey of life. It's been a journey indeed. I appreciate my spiritual leaders, mentors, fathers and mothers, my business associates, my academic colleagues, and all the friends who, in one way or the other, have contributed to shaping the man I have become now in God.

I will make a mention of a few because of time and space. Mr. Emmanuel Bolum through whom I came to Christ and the preliminary knowledge about God; Rev Bayo

ACKNOWLEDGMENT

Adenugba through whom the Lord baptized me into the spirit of the prophetic and the apostolic; Isaac Okorie, Apostle Victor Uchegbulam through whom God trained me in the place of prayer; Pastor Paul Ogedengbe, Dr. Noel Woodroof, Rick Joyner, John Eckhardt, through whose books and lifestyles I got sustained in the apostolic and the present emphasis of the Spirit; Pastor Taiwo Lemoshe, Pastor Demola Adesona, Rev Blessing Igbokwe, for your encouragement and support in life; Tunde Soetan, Isaac Arikawe, Wale Odeniyi, Dotun Oluwagbohun, for friendly advice, relationship and fellowship; brother Falu and Mama Margaret of River of Life, Houston TX and the entire members of the community.

Great thanks to the staff of the Rehoboth House, *AKA* Kingdom Publishers, for an impressive work on this book, from editing to the finishing. What an excellent piece.

There are lots of friends, colleagues, and associates whose names are not mentioned here. It does not mean that you are less important, No. My God will reward every one of you beyond my highest prayers in Jesus' name. Amen.

PRINCIPLES FOR BUILDING IN THE KINGDOM

Endorsement

What a treatise the Lord has moved His son, Tony, to write to the (The Body Of Christ) Church. This is an accurate dissection of the word, precept upon precept and line upon line. We should prayerfully read this book, as it sets us on the right path to building according to the principles of the Kingdom. It's either we are building rightly, according to God's pattern, or wrongly according to the world's pattern. With whatever pattern we build, our work shall be tested either by fire or by flood to reveal the quality and how it was built.

This book addresses salient issues in the Body of Christ today and will help to realign us with the heart of the Father.

I endorse it and pray that the same Spirit that moved our brother to write this book will profoundly touch and stir our hearts to build according to God's Kingdom principles.

God has blessed you.

Taiwo Lemoshe,
Senior Pastor,
God's Chamber Ministries,
Lagos, Nigeria.

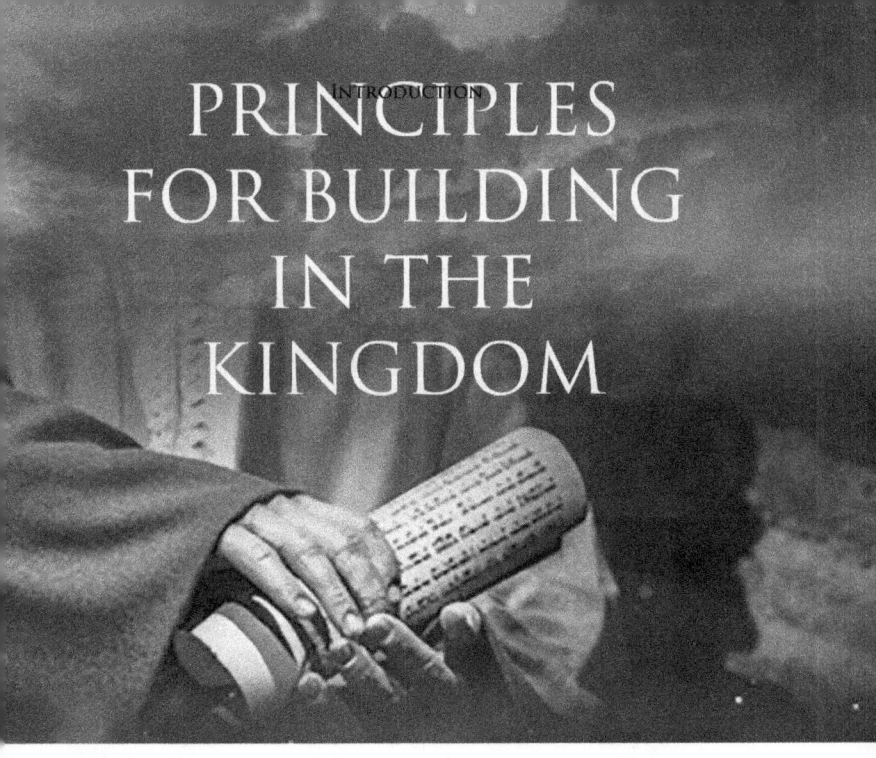

PRINCIPLES FOR BUILDING IN THE KINGDOM

Introduction

The word building is construction terminology. It requires a process and needs time to accomplish. Typically, the project owner will engage the services of different professionals and skilled workers to translate his design into a physical structure that stands out. Although the term building is often related to houses and other physical structures, it can represent every other aspect of life.

Though human beings build but the builder of all things is God. He builds our lives to His taste and standards so that He can live in us. We are a building in His hands that requires a process of time to complete in phases. God, who is the master builder, has the blueprint of our lives with a detailed plan. He builds according to the pattern in the blueprint. This scripture referenced below in Ephesians further explained it.

> *"For we are his workmanship, created in Christ Jesus unto good works, which God hath before ordained that we should walk in them" (Eph 2:10, NKJ).*

The builder of all things is God.
He designs the blueprint of our lives, how we ought to live.

All we do is to play it out as planned.

What a building plan is in the hand of a builder is what our life's plans and activities are in the hands of our builder – the Lord Jesus, who determines the direction of our lives and how we should navigate through the issues of life. Because our lives are a metaphor of a building under divine construction, there are different processes and stages of growth we go through in our daily lives. This building is shaped by the various people and experiences God allows us to interact with every day of our lives.

Many may start life at the same time and place but end up differently. Two people can be born by the same parents, and one ends up being a responsible and successful entrepreneur who loves God and respects people, while the other ends up a miscreant and an ungodly person.

Much more, two people can also start well in life on a level playing field, and at the end of the day, one is satisfied and fulfilled because God approved his work, while the other is not because God never approved his work. The reason being that the latter did not build according to the pattern of life ordained for him by God. Cain and Abel are typical examples of this scenario.

When God demanded an offering from them, Cain and Abel brought offerings out of the produce of their effort. However, God rejected Cain's offering and accepted Abel's offering. In Gen 4:7, God gave the reason why He did not accept Cain's offering. He said Cain did not 'do well.' To 'do well' in this context in Hebrews means 'yatab,' which means to make one's course line up with that which is pleasing to God and that which is well-pleasing in His sight.

The issue with Cain was not his sacrifice, as many think but for himself. It was the issue of personal alignment. He was not aligned with God's purpose.

With this in mind, it becomes imperative that the principles guiding our growth process should be adequately taught and well understood. It is not enough to build but to build in a manner that will receive a **'well done, good and worthy servant'** commendation from our Maker and Builder—The Lord Jesus Christ. Matt 25: 21,23.

> **God designs our lives, but we can choose
> to follow His ways or follow our soulish path;
> whichever, we will face the consequence of our actions**

In building technology, a builder builds for ratification. The building will not be approved if the builder fails to build according to the architectural blueprint, regardless of how aesthetic it looks. Taking this building as a project, the builder works closely with the project owner according to the building plan. Imagine that the project owner wants a one-story building, but the builder feels it's better to build a two-story building without the project owner's approval, irrespective of his effort and intelligence; the project will not get the owner's support. When a building is built according to the approved blueprint, the owner puts his **approval and acceptance seal**. The seal of acceptance in the building of our lives is the Lord Jesus Christ.

> **In whatever we build or present before God,
> Jesus Christ is the seal of His acceptance. God wants
> to see His Son in everything we do on earth.
> That is His divine approval**

There are principles upon which we build anything that will receive approval from God and stands the test of time. These principles are discovered in Hebrews 11: 13-15.

> *"These all died in faith, not having received the promises, but having seen them afar off, and were persuaded of them, and*

embraced them, and confessed that they were strangers and pilgrims on the earth; for they that say such things declare plainly that they seek a country, and truly if they had been mindful of that country from where they had come from, they would have had opportunity to have returned."

This scripture's background story is about the lifestyle of our fathers of old called the heroes of faith. Notice also that the scripture also mentioned women among these outstanding believers. This scripture teaches us about the principles and patterns that made them successful in their walk with God on the earth.

"All Scripture is inspired by God and is useful to teach us what is true and make us realize what is wrong in our lives. It corrects us when we are wrong and teaches us to do what is right. God uses it to prepare and equip his people to do every good work" (II Tim3:16-17, NLT).

We want to trust the Holy Spirit to teach us the right architecture in building what will last and receive approval from God as **well done, my faithful servant."**

These Are The Principles Outlined From The Above Scripture.

(a) **Vision**: Having seen them afar off
(b) **Persuasion**: Persuaded of them
(c) **Embrace**: Embraced them
(d) **Confession:** Confessed that they were strangers and pilgrims on earth

I will further explain these principles in detail in subsequent chapters as they form the core content of this book.

The purpose of this book is to help us realize that our lives, careers, and all of life's endeavors are buildings before our Maker. It is not just enough to build in whatever capacity and discipline we find ourselves but to build in the WAY AND PATTERN God ordained for us. God has ordained principles and patterns that every building must undergo to receive His approval, irrespective of its nature, capacity, or magnitude.

From the time God speaks to man to accomplish a purpose to the time the purpose is achieved, a gap must be filled for that word to come to pass. We need to go through stages and processes for that assignment to receive a well-done commendation from the Lord.

In this book, we will learn what we need to know and do to get God's kind of success in His word over our lives.

It is not enough to grow or build our lives, our ministries, our destinies, or whatever we feel God wants us to build here on earth; it must be built in a way that will receive a **'well done, good and worthy servant'** from our Maker and Builder—The Lord Jesus Christ.

INTRODUCTION

It is my prayer that as you read this book, the Lord will give you understanding and wisdom like a wise master builder to apply the principles outlined in it so you can build accurately and powerfully on the earth.

PRINCIPLES FOR BUILDING IN THE KINGDOM

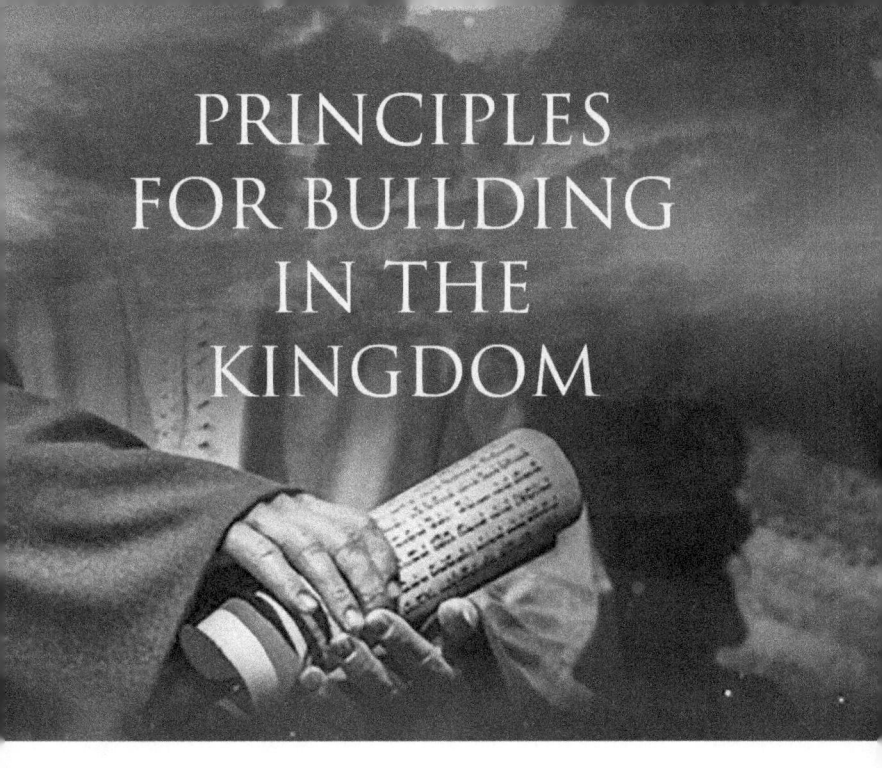

PRINCIPLES FOR BUILDING IN THE KINGDOM

CHAPTER 1

Building In The Accurate Way

Building a house or some form of activity or life has some processes involved. It also requires some level of professionalism, strategy, and tactics. In essence, it needs a direction (blueprint or plan that the builder must adhere to). It requires a great deal of time to plan and strategize before any work can commence.

A gigantic edifice can collapse overnight if the foundation is faulty. The cost of rebuilding it can never be compared with the initial cost of planning and building according to the original pattern.

> *"Prepare thy works without, and make it fit for thyself in the field, and afterward build thy house" (Prov. 24: 27).*

This scripture talks of preparation before starting to build. Preparation is crucial that it cannot be overemphasized. Architectural design and the **cost of the building are the** two main things a builder must arm himself with during preparation.

Architectural Design: The architectural design helps the builder see the big picture and understands the details of the building. He knows how big or small the building is. Some of us live the way we see our lives per day. Because of no foresight, some don't have the big picture of their lives' ultimate destiny and purpose and hence no motivation or drive to push through to the end. Unfortunately, building without motivation and commitment to finish will eventually lead to abandoning the building when confronted with life's challenges and look for an alternative because of not having the whole picture in mind.

Cost Of The Building: With this, the builder knows how to source the required funds for the building. Some of us don't see the cost implications of most adventures we undertake. We are so much in a hurry to arrive at the end that we ignore calculating the cost. Let me point it clear to us that doing the will of God has many cost implications. Suppose all we see in our destiny's path is the gigantic building (the achieved success, the result, or the finality of our endeavor) when challenges come during our building process. In that case, we will back out for not fully grasping the cost implication.

Read what Paul wrote in one of the epistles.

> *"Yea doubtless, and I count all things but loss for the excellency of the knowledge of Christ Jesus my Lord: for whom I have suffered the loss of all things, and do count them but dung, that I may win Christ" (Phil 3:8).*

In the course of God's building in Apostle Paul's life, he had to calculate his loss and counted all of them as dung so that he might win Christ. Building lives is a serious matter. Imagine a man who has lived all his life pursuing a goal that is not his, built empires, and at the time of reward, he was told that he never did anything because none of those things was counted for him. What a significant loss.

Building life in God's pattern is a serious business. It is all that God has brought us here to do and must not be done with levity or slothfulness. Every attention is required to avoid collapse.

Take a look at **Matt 7:22-23** in different versions of the Bible.

> "Many will say to Me in that day, 'Lord, Lord, have we not prophesied in Your name, cast out demons in Your name, and done many wonders in Your name?' And then I will declare to them, 'I never knew you; depart from Me, <u>you who practice lawlessness</u>!" (NKJV).
>
> "I can see it now-at the Final Judgment thousands strutting up to me and saying, 'Master, we preached the Message, we bashed the demons, our God-sponsored projects had everyone talking.' And do you know what I am going to say? 'You missed the boat. <u>All you did was use me to make yourselves important.</u> You don't impress me one bit. You're out of here" (THE MESSAGE).
>
> "On judgment day, many will say to me, 'Lord! Lord! We prophesied in your name and cast out demons in your name and performed many miracles in your name.' But I will reply, 'I never knew you. Get away from me, <u>you who break God's laws</u>" (NLT).
>
> "At the Judgment, many will tell me, 'Lord, Lord, we told others about you and used your name to cast out demons and to do many other great miracles.' But I will reply, <u>'You have never been mine. Go away, for your deeds are evil</u>" (TLB).

Analytical study of these scriptures shows that our Lord Jesus was not talking about people who do not understand Him. Notice that they could prophesy, heal the sick, wrought miracles and preach good messages in His name. But why will our Lord Jesus say to them, *"I never knew you."* They were not using the Lord's name in vain, and it was not counterfeit, so if these people have grown to have gotten these powers to do these works, they may not be babes in the Lord. The Lord Jesus said He never knew them. The word "knew" here has the same root meaning as the one used for intercourse. *"Adam knew his wife, and they brought forth a son."*

Jesus explained that those people never had a relationship with Him to produce those seeds (miracles), so their works were not recorded on their accounts in heaven. This means the seed that produced the results never came from the Lord. They only used God to achieve relevance and create a name for themselves. They built their destiny, but not according to the pattern set for them. There was never an internal union with the Creator of destiny.

Luke Chapter captures these thoughts very well:

> *"Strive to enter by the narrow door, for many, I tell you, will seek to enter and will not be able. Once the head of the house gets up and shuts the door, and you begin to stand outside and knock on the door, saying, 'Lord, open up to us!' then He will answer and say to you, **'I do not know where you are from.'** Then you will begin to say, <u>'We ate and drank in Your presence, and You taught in our streets; and He will say,' I tell you; I do not know where you are from; depart from Me, all you evildoers.'</u> There will be weeping and gnashing of teeth there when you see Abraham and*

Isaac and Jacob and all the prophets in the kingdom of God, but yourselves being cast out. And they will come from east and west, and from north and south, and will recline at the table in the kingdom of God. And behold, some are last who will be first, and some are first who will be last" (**Luke 13:24-30**, *NASB).*

The word "strive" means that a lot of effort and energy is needed to press into the kingdom. There will be many disappointments on that day. Some will eat and drink from the presence of the Lord, yet they are not qualified to enter. Some would have heard the good word of the Lord with great anointing, yet they never acted in line with God's purpose for their lives. You can receive great miracles from the Lord, yet your life is not in line with His purpose.

When people were calling onto the Lord, He said He does not know where they are from. That means He cannot locate them on His spiritual radar. They never existed according to His plans and purpose for their lives. They lived by their own will. They only gave pleasure to themselves even though they were following the Lord, eating and drinking from God's presence. All through their stay with the Lord Jesus, His seed was never planted in them. They were with Jesus but not of Him (no fellowship). They were lawless people who never obeyed the pathways God ordained for them. They served God as it suited them. Their purpose was not divinely sourced.

They were <u>with Jesus;</u> hence they did many miracles in His name. Unfortunately, they were not <u>of Jesus</u>.

> *"They went out from us, but they were not of us; for if they had been of us, they would no doubt have continued with us: but they went out, that they might be made manifest that they were not all of us." (I John 2:19).*

Being with Jesus can produce miracles, signs, and wonders without His personality being built in us. But being of Jesus produces His character, nature, and goodwill, which eventually will produce every other manifestation of God needed. It will also direct how to utilize them to profit God and bless humanity maximally.

If Jesus does not acknowledge people who did great works for God just because they did not follow the divine plan, it signals that serious attention should be placed on the building and what and how we build. For no other foundation can any man lay except that which has been laid, which is Jesus Christ.

Kenneth Hagin (Snr.) of the blessed memory in his book,' Purpose, Plan and Pursuit' said he worked for 12 years as an Evangelist with thousands of souls saved and many miracles performed. However, God told him none of those works was recorded for him because that was not his purpose. He was doing what God did not assign him to do.

Jesus not acknowledging people who did great works for God just because they did not follow the divine plan draws earnest attention, not to only the building but what and how we build.

Build According To Pattern

"And see to it that you make them according to the pattern which was shown you on the mountain" (Ex 25:40, NKJV).

This scripture highlights the importance of building according to God's design. We can see the instruction God gave to Moses to build the tabernacle and its instruments and arrangement of the priestly garments. God designated a significant part of the Book of Exodus to analyze the accurate measurements, sizes, and colors of the holy things He assigned to Moses. God took enough time to describe the building's details. Intermittently, He will remind Moses to be careful to follow all the instructions He has shown him on the mount. He got a man by the name Bezaleel, filled with the wisdom of God, to design Aaron's garment. God is not just interested in a garment but a particular garment of His type.

God instructed Noah when building the Ark for the saving of his household. He gave detailed instructions on how to construct the Ark. What made the Ark sail on the top of the waters and the tabernacle, and the holy things to receive God's approval was not because they were meticulously built but because Noah and Moses built strictly under God's instructions. All that is good may all not be God's. It must be God's before it can be pronounced good.

> *"Now, this I do for the gospel's sake that I may partake of it with you. Do you not know that those who run in a race all run, but one receives the prize? Run in such a way that you may obtain it. Everyone who competes for the prize is temperate in all things. Now they do it to obtain a perishable crown, but we for an imperishable crown. Therefore I run thus: not with <u>uncertainty</u>. Thus I fight: <u>not as one who beats the air. But I discipline my body and bring it into subjection, lest when I have preached to others, I myself should become disqualified</u>"* (I Cor 9: 23-27, NKJV).

I have feared this scripture the most in my walk with the Lord. Each time I read it, I always wonder in fear of my motives and actions. Everybody can run, preach, give alms, do all manner of good works in the name of the Lord, but not all of that will receive the prize (approval from God). This scripture says there is a way (pattern) you have to run to obtain it.

God gave specific and detailed instructions for building the tabernacle, the sowing of the priestly garments and the building of Noah's Ark because of their importance. God has given specific instructions concerning your life, so you must follow them accordingly.

You must be temperate in all your motives and actions. To be temperate means you have to exercise regulated control of your emotions and actions. You don't do things because you like to do them or because some people are doing them. You must receive the instruction from above. This regulated lifestyle is not compulsory for everyone but for those who want to receive the imperishable crown from the Lord on the day of reckoning. There is the need for discipline, without which after building an empire for God or doing great and marvelous things that deserve appreciation, you get a disqualification.

> **God does not respond to peoples' cries that have no link to His word or His principles. He is a principled God who judges issues based on His word.**

God is a principled God. He does not respond to people's cry that has no link to His word or His principles. The world cries to God for various reasons, asking for help, healing, prosperity, breakthroughs, yet God doesn't just answer everyone. He responds to His word, not because He loves or hates you. God watches over His word to perform them. The Psalmist in Psalm 103:20 declared how God pays rapt attention to His words in the mouth of His saints.

> *"Bless the Lord, you His angels, who excel in strength, who do his commandments, heeding to the voice of his word."*

The strength of a believer is in heeding the voice of His word. His joy and satisfaction in the works He gave us produce the strength we need to move on in life. If we must build what will stand the test of time, we must build according to the pattern (blueprint) God has designed for it. Whether our lives, business empires, political institutions, academic pursuits, or kingdom investments, they must be built with a set pattern to receive God's approval.

In this age of apostolic reformation, God is raising builders, pioneers, and saints that will build new structures to accommodate the new initiatives God is unveiling on earth today. The typical language in the apostolic atmosphere is building: rebuilding the lost glory; rebuilding the temple of worship; rebuilding the altar of prayer; rebuilding the systems and structures of authority in the earth. It is entirely a whole new day of rebuilding the ruins of the Tabernacle of David.

> **The typical language in the atmosphere of the apostolic is building.**

There are indicators to measure if a work is done according to God's instructions or not. It is possible to assume God's approval in what we build, not realizing that there is no God in it, even when people say that God is there. Do not be misled by human accolades.

The Old Testament told us of a king who did what was right in the sight of the Lord but not with a perfect heart.

> *"Amaziah was twenty-five years old when he became king, and he reigned in Jerusalem twenty-nine years. His mother's name was Jehoaddan; she was from Jerusalem. <u>He did what was right in the eyes of the Lord, but not wholeheartedly</u>" (II Chron 25:2, NIV).*

One will wonder how one can serve the Lord very well but not with a right (perfect) heart. Will God approve that work? The issue here is the heart and not the activities. Our motives count more than our actions. God judges the heart and not primarily our actions. Two people can do the right thing but with different motives. In the realm of the spirit, our thoughts (motives) speak louder than our actions. After God created man, He gave him the right of choice. We decide what we make of the life that God gave to us, either to follow God's pattern or an alternative.

Dear beloved, as you read this book, I pray that the Spirit of God will prompt you to turn a new life so that your work will receive approval from Him. Amen.

In the realm of the spirit, our thoughts (motives) speak louder than our actions.

The Acid Test Of Our Building

> *"Therefore whoever hears these sayings of Mine, and does them, I will liken him to a wise man who built his home on the rock, and the rain descended, the floods came, and*

the wind blew and beat on that house; and it did not fall, for it was founded on the rock. But everyone who hears these sayings of Mine, and does not do them, will be like a foolish man who built his house on the sand: and the rain descended, the floods came, and the winds blew and beat on that house, and it fell. And great was its fall' (Matt 7: 24-27).

"Whoever comes to Me and hears My sayings and does them, I will show you whom he is like: he is like a man building a house, who dug deep and laid the foundation on the rock. And when the flood arose, the stream beat vehemently against that house and could not shake it, for it was founded on the rock. But he who heard and did nothing is like a man who built a house on the earth without foundation, against which the stream beat vehemently, and immediately it fell. And the ruin of that house was great" (Luke 6: 47-49).

In determining the pattern and tenacity of what we are building, some of the things we build will collapse as we take our journey to the end of the age. This is because, on that day, each building will be tested by these three values: **RAIN, FLOOD,** and **WIND**. Beloved every building (whatever we do on earth in any field of human endeavor, irrespective of our religious inclination) will pass through the test of these three things. This process will ultimately determine what becomes of our labor here on earth.

The same values: RAIN, FLOOD, and WIND are used to evaluate every person's work on earth, which determines what becomes of our labor, irrespective of one's discipline or religious inclination.

In the scriptures above, you will notice that the three values mentioned affected both buildings: the one built on the rock and the one built on sand. The buildings represent our activities on earth and prove that these values are the acid test for accurately building anything in God in this life. These acid tests will test our ministry, lifestyle, purpose, marriage and family, career, and everything we do on earth.

> **The three values are the acid test to our ministry, lifestyle, purpose, marriage and family, career, and all we do on earth.**

What is the implication of the rain, the flood, and the wind (storm) in our lives, as it relates to what we build? These are activities that reveal what is inside of us as we progress on our journey in God. **Lk 2:35** says, ***"A sword shall pierce through your own soul and that the thoughts of many hearts shall be revealed."*** When these values pierce through us like a sword, the hidden intention of our hearts shall be revealed.

The Lord is the one sending those values: - the rain, the flood, and the storm upon humanity to test whether what we are building can stand the test or not. He sends rain both to the righteous and the unrighteous.

"...He causes his sun to rise on the evil and the good and sends rain on the righteous and the unrighteous" (Matt 5:45, NIV).

Times of crisis, turbulence, and darkness is coming upon the earth more than ever. As these pierce through the souls of men and examine all that we do in life, our true inward personality will manifest outwardly. Take a look at this scripture below.

"For we are God's fellow workers; you are God's field, you are God's building. According to the grace of God which was given to me, as a wise master builder, I have laid the foundation, and another builds on it. But let each one take heed of how he builds on it. For no other foundation can anyone lay than that which is laid, which is Jesus Christ. Now if anyone builds on this foundation with gold, silver, precious stones, wood, hay, straw, each one's work will become clear; for the day will declare it, because it will be revealed by fire; and the fire will test each one's work, of what sort it is. If anyone's work which he has built on it endures, he will receive a reward. If anyone's work is burned, he will suffer loss; but he himself will be saved, yet so as through fire!" (I Cor. 3:9-15).

Some build with gold, silver, and precious stones, while others build with wood, hay, and straw. Whichever material you build with, the determining factor to whether it will be accepted or not is the fire. The fire of God is manifested through these values, which typified the period of crisis.

The implication is that we could be scarcely saved, but our labor and effort would be gone, and we lose our rewards. There will be many disappointments, crying, and weeping because of the unexpected and enormous loss some of us will suffer.

A pastor with a big cathedral can lose all the labor because of building wrongly, though he might be saved in the end. The darkness spoken of in the book of Isaiah 60:2 is an example. It will affect every building, but the one built on the rock will produce light at the end of the day.

> *"See, darkness covers the earth, and thick darkness is over the peoples, but the Lord rises upon you, and his glory appears over you" (Isaiah 60:2).*

Times of crisis, turbulence, and darkness is coming upon the earth more than ever. As these pierce through the souls of men and examine all that we do in life, our true inward personality will manifest outwardly.

God promised that He would shake the earth and the heavens and the things that are in them. These shakings will bring a clear demarcation of who we are. Our foundation may be on the rock, but what we build can fail the fire test, and we lose our reward. Nonetheless, we will be saved but will lose our reward. It would have been better we never worked at all.

The essence of this book is to protect whatever we are building, so they don't get burnt up at the end, and we lose our reward. The following scriptures discuss the Lord stirring up the shakings such as tsunami, hurricane, vortex, earthquake, famine, socio-economic and religious crisis.

> *"Whose voice then shook the earth; but now He has promised saying. "yet once more I shake not only the earth but also the heavens" Now this yet once more indicates the removal of those things that are being shaken, as of things that are made, that the things which cannot be shaken may remain. Therefore, since we are receiving a kingdom that cannot be shaken, let us have grace by which we may serve God acceptably with reverence and godly fear. For our, God is a consuming fire" (Heb 12:26-29).*

> *"For thus says the Lord of hosts: Once more (it is a little while) I will shake heaven and the earth, the sea and drylands, and I shake all nations, and they shall come to the Desire of All Nations, and I will fill this temple with glory, says the lord of hosts" (Hagg. 2:6-7).*

> *"The Lord also will roar from Zion, and utter the voice from Jerusalem; the heavens and the earth will shake, but the Lord will be a shelter for His people, and the strength of the children of Israel" (Joel 3:16:).*

The test starts with rain, then graduates to flood, and then to storm (heavy wind).

Structures Built On Rock Or Sand

From the above scriptures- **Matt 7:24-27 and 1Cor. 3:9-15**; the foundation of any building can either be deepened with rock or sand. Structures built on rock will stand, while those built on sand will fall. We must understand what these rocks or sand represent in our building.

Rock: This symbolizes a solid foundation whose stand is based on a gripe. This gripe is found in dependency on Jesus, the Chief Builder. It also represents divine revelation coming from the throne room of heaven.

We define rock as a rigid solid material that forms parts of the earth's surface. It has different shapes and sizes, indicating the uniqueness of purpose. Buildings built with rocks are unique, each drawing inspiration and revelation from the Lord Jesus – the source. No two rocks (stone) are exactly alike, showing that no two works (building) in God are the same, eradicating rivalry and competition.

Sand: This symbolizes humanistic reasoning that seeks to get a name for itself. Examples of this type of building are the tower of Babel in Gen 11 and the golden image of King Nebuchadnezzar of Babylon in Dan 3. Most of the buildings here have many similarities as they come from the initiative of men. Businesses, organizations, marriages, and any pursuit built to seek power, wealth, or fame outside

God's dependency is built on sand. It doesn't matter if you are a pastor, bishop, or pope; neither does it matter how much revenue you generate from the business.

These two systems become the two areas upon which all that man builds on earth is done. It is either rock (stone) system that takes you to Zion or sand (block) system which takes you to Babylon. We can analyze whatever we do in the context of these two parallel operations.

Judging from the scriptures above, what we build on the rock or sand can stand for a while, but the most durable ones are on the rock. They may not be any noticeable difference between the two types of building, or even sometimes the ones built on sand may seem (look) glamorous and gorgeous, but when the acid test of fire comes, it reveals the difference.

Buildings (businesses, organizations, marriages, families, and any pursuit) built with rock represent uniqueness drawing inspiration and revelation from the Lord Jesus-the source. In contrast, buildings constructed with sand represent self-seeking, power, wealth, or fame outside of God's dependency.

Comparison Of Buildings On Rock And Sand	
It leads to Zionic order; heavenly system	It leads to Babylonic order; earthly system
It's a product of revelation (divinely sourced from God)	It's a product of human reasoning (earthly inspired by man)
This is spiritual and divine	This is carnal and sensual
Based on a solid (robust) foundation	Based on a weak (porous) foundation
It seeks a name and glory for God and His Kingdom	Seek a name for self glorification
Each stone is unique, showing originality	Each block is identical, showing imitation
It leads to a life of complement and orderliness	It leads to a life of rivalry and competition

The subsequent chapters will detail the different principles that govern what we build and examine if they will receive God's approval or not. It is my prayer that God will open your eyes to see and hear His words in the pages of this book in Jesus name.

PRINCIPLES FOR BUILDING IN THE KINGDOM

CHAPTER 2

Building Principle One: Vision

"And these all died in faith, not having received the promise, but having seen them afar off, and were persuaded of them, and embraced them and confessed that they were strangers and pilgrims on the earth" (Heb 11:13).

Having gone through the rudiments and mechanics of building accurately in the introduction and chapter one, we need to dive deeper into those principles required to build excellently. There are four fundamental principles, and each is discussed in the subsequent four chapters. We will discuss these four essential principles in more detail. Chapter six will carefully examine the hindrances to building excellently and conclude with a clarion call for a reawakening to build in chapter 7. Please, patiently come along with me as we begin to prod into each of them.

As the above scripture says, "These all died in faith, not having received the promises, but having seen them afar off. This talks of vision – the ability to see from afar. The Greek meaning of seeing from afar is 'Eido,' which means to see, know by perception, behold, look, be aware, consider, to know, be sure, understand, and have divine knowledge.

To build accurately, we must first see the building in the spirit so we can replicate it here on earth. God is Spirit, and we have to be in the spirit to see what He is instructing us to build. No meaningful life can be lived for God, nor can any significant work be done for Him unless it is firmly grounded in the spiritual reality of the vision.

> **No meaningful life can be lived for God, nor can any significant work be done for Him unless it is firmly grounded in the spiritual reality of the vision.**

What Is Divine Vision?

Simply put, divine vision is the revelation God gives to a person about what He intends to do.

From this definition, divine vision is not a man's idea. It is not a burden or the good or godly things we desire to achieve for God. It is not about aspiring to be rich so we can use the money to sponsor the gospel. It is not about the desire to help the poor and the needy. It is not what we perceive that needs to be done or what we want to accomplish for the Kingdom of God. All of these are good and noble, but they are not a vision from God. Instead, divine vision is a divinely inspired directive that evokes a response and provokes us to act. It is a product of God working in us. The vision of the Lord consumes and summons us.

> **Divine vision is not the desire to help the poor and the needy or what we perceive needs to be done or what we want to accomplish for the Kingdom of God.**

God's given vision is what lifts a man from obscurity to stardom and enables him to achieve incredible things for God. Vision from God changed the lives of most of the notable characters in the Bible, e.g., Abraham, Moses, David, Isaiah, Jeremiah, Paul, to mention a few. These Bible characters had encounters with God which were more involved than personal revelation. They had a word from God deeply rooted in their lives and triggered a lifetime of service and direction for God. All the people whom God mightily used have a life-changing encounter with Him. It was as if God was trying to get their undivided attention to listen to Him and whole-heartedly obey Him for the rest of their lives. The spiritual vision these people received from God took hold of them and set them up for life. All they passionately did was to serve the vision God gave them.

We can also define vision as a revelation of a realistic, credible, attractive future for an individual, an organization, or a generation. Vision is foresight, based on insight with the benefit of hindsight. It is the act of seeing the invisible and a clear mental picture of a glorious future. To have a divine vision, you must first have a functional relationship with the giver of the vision – The Lord Jesus Christ.

> **Divine vision is a divinely inspired directive that evokes a response and provokes us to act.**

According to Charles Swindoll, 'vision is essential for survival- It is spawned by faith, sustained by hope, sparked by imagination and strengthened by enthusiasm. It is greater than sight, deeper than a dream, broader than an idea'. A vision encompasses vast vistas outside the realm of the predictable, the safe, and the expected. No wonder we perish without it.

> *"Where there is no prophetic vision (revelation), the people perish (cast off restraint); but he that keeps the law, happy (blessed) is he" (Prov. 29:18, ESV).*

For any work or ministry to be fulfilled or receive God's approval, it must first be seen. There must be a blueprint from heaven. It must be clear and distinct without any ambiguity. This sight comes through a divine relationship with God and what He is doing on earth. It must be a vision birthed by prophetic revelation from God.

Divine vision comes through a divine relationship with God and what He is doing on earth.

Having a vision from God does not exclusively mean being a pastor or having a pulpit ministry. Every work that will receive God's approval must come through divine vision. A man who receives instructions from God to sell foodstuffs so that people don't suffer hunger is preserving lives that will serve God. This is a vision from God. Such a person will unquestionably be blessed from his business venture and receive God's approval of a fulfilled life. That is what will count for him on the last day. Everybody has a gift (talent) to profit all. God will reward you based on your faithfulness of that gift towards God and His people. It is the gift you received from God that is called vision. A person who has the vision to be a farmer, an engineer, an artisan, a medical doctor, or any other profession from God is not less fulfilled or essential than a pulpit pastor whom God calls. They are all called by God to fulfill a particular part of God's universal agenda on earth. In Ephesians 4:1, Apostle Paul called the people to walk worthy of the vocation wherein they have been called. The word vocation is more of a business terminology than a religious expression. That word is interchangeably used with 'calling' in some versions of the Bible. Double-check the King James Version (KJV) and the New King James Version (NKJV).

Please look out for my book "**Ministry: The Release of Life**" for more details of who and what it means to minister to the Lord.

> **God's call today is not limited to pastoral or pulpit ministry alone; God is calling people into every field of human endeavor to fill the earth with His glory as He has promised.**

Vision is God's intent communicated into the heart (spirit) of man. Michael Faraday's discoveries of electromagnetic induction and the laws of electrolysis were God's intent to make the world a better habitat for man. God put this idea into the heart of a man who fulfilled it, and it became a blessing to the entire human race. The discovery of antibiotics to cure humans of sicknesses and diseases is God's intent to preserve life. Every person has a vocation or calling from God. God brought us here to accomplish something unique as part of His overall program on earth. Everyone is a piece of the puzzle.

God desires man to function perfectly on earth in every aspect of life: spirit, soul, and body. The vision He puts in our hearts is the avenue through which He unveils His universal agenda for mankind. The vision God gave to the Pharaoh of Egypt in Joseph's time was His plan to end starvation on earth at the time. Whenever man cooperates with God and responds to that divine call, and does our part of the deal, it unleashes God's ability combined with our efforts to solve global problems confronting the human race.

It's like an ecosystem, where every individual is a significant piece, contributing their quota given by the Lord. When the entire ecosystem is in order, we can achieve the equilibrium intended by God from the beginning of time.

> *"This is the thing which I have spoken to Pharaoh. God has shown Pharaoh what He is about to do" (Gen 41:28, NKJV).*

Egypt sold the food to sustain life and solve the imminent global starvation at the time. It became the food basket of the then world. God can call you to start a business to serve different needs, and as you provide those services or products, you will be earning money.

How To Birth A Divine Vision

Since we have established that divine vision is a revelation of God to man, it will require God and man's effort to fulfill a vision. God is willing to release the vision, but man must be ready and willing to receive it. It is a functional relationship between a man and God. God creates the vision, and as we receive it into our lives, it becomes a rallying point or a goal that we pursue as His people. The questions are not, "where do "I" want to go?' Or "what do "I" want to become?," but "where does "He" wants to take me to?" and what does "He" wants me to do or become?"

> **Vision is a product of a functional relationship between a man and God and what He is doing on earth.**

A vision from God can be seen, heard, experienced. It can be personal and prophetic. It can also come through a dream, an intuition, an open vision, or an idea. We are to have an open mind while approaching God to reveal His mind about our destiny. God reveals that His vision for our lives is in His time, not ours. So, we simply need to get on with life, obeying Him and living to pleases Him until He shows up. God's revelation has an appointed time for each one of us.

> *"For the vision is yet for an appointed time, But at the end, it will speak, and it will not lie. Though it tarries, wait for it; Because it will surely come, It will not tarry" (Haba.2:3, NKJV).*

Moses was 80 years old when he received his corporate vision from God. Many years before this, he seemed to have had an idea of what God wanted him to do, but that was a personal vision, which was not yet time to be unveiled in God's calendar. Our job is to preserve the vision until we are matured and complete, not lacking anything. We are to be continuously opened to God so that He can explain His will to us in phases.

> *"But let patience have its perfect work, that you may be [a] perfect and complete, lacking nothing" (James 1:4, NKJV).*

How To Determine If A Vision Is From God Or Not

Not all vision comes from God. A vision may come from self, from the devil, from the burden in our hearts or the needs around us. We must be able to differentiate when God speaks. Any ministry, vision, or idea from God must express the personality of Christ. Here are some points though not exhaustive, of how to know if a vision is from the Lord or not.

The God-given vision must be bigger than you (the recipient), so you can seek mercy and grace from God: Whatever vision God gives, He wants to be part of fulfilling it. But if it is what you can easily handle, you may not need Him. God cannot give you a vision that your ability, finance, and wherewithal alone can cope. All the notable Bible characters received visions that compelled them to continue returning to God for more explanations, direction, insight, and help in every area. You need the giver of the vision to fulfill the vision.

A God-given vision can be given to a person, but it is meant for a people: God's vision should never benefit an individual alone. No matter the vision you receive from God, it must benefit others and bring glory to God. God's mind is not about a person but a vast majority of people. Whatever God does on earth, He has the whole world in mind. The Bible says the mind of God is full of Man (the world as a whole). When He calls a man, He has a nation in mind.

A God-given vision must produce salvation and redemption: There is one key reason why God is interested in humanity. It is to draw them back to Himself for His glory and pleasure. So any vision or activity we have that does not reflect His glory and pleasure is not of God, no matter how impressive it may seem.

How can a peasant, a farmer, a trader, or any other profession considered a vision from God lead people to salvation and redemption? The first point to note here is that all these vocations are ministries. As we relate with our customers with God's values in us, we impact their lives with the quality of God's life that will make them see God in us. Joseph in Egypt influenced the entire nation with the godly attributes in him without being religious. You need to read my other book 'Ministry- The Release of Life.' It dealt extensively on this subject.

A God-given vision must draw you up to Him: We can't have an encounter with God, receive His vision, and afterward remain the same. That cannot be a vision from God. Any vision from God summons us to Him and demands a response from Him. You can be the most generous philanthropist in human history, but if your life never changed positively towards God, your philanthropic ministry cannot be a vision from God. You can receive men's approval and accolade but not God's.

> **Not all visions come from God.**
> **A vision may come from self, from the devil,**
> **from the burden in your heart, or the needs around you.**
> **You must differentiate between when God speaks or not.**

Effects Of A God-Given Vision

It Is Quickening: It brings life because it provides a life-changing thrust that brings new direction and purpose to our lives. Our lives may have been heading in one direction, but once we receive God's vision, it grips us, and we can do nothing but change direction and serve God's purpose. Dr. Martin Luther King Jr. could not stop but persisted in the liberation of the black race in America even when it was detrimental to his life and family's wellbeing.

It Is Motivating: Any vision from God can enable us to advance towards the implicit goals within it. If we have no vision from God, we stagnate and perish. A vision from God carries the seed of God's purpose for our lives and the people destined for the vision. God's vision comes with the knowledge that we can fulfill our part because God will provide us with everything we need. We should also know that God will not have called us if we don't have what it takes in Him to fulfill our part of the bargain.

It Is Constraining: Those who have indeed received God's vision into their hearts only do things that align with that vision. They separate themselves from their old way of life, desiring to please God at all cost and enable the vision they have received from Him. God gave Noah the vision to build an Ark with divine specifications to strictly obey. So also was Moses when God said he should be careful to observe to do all that He showed him on the mount. Vision defines who we are, what we do, and those we relate with.

It Is Sanctifying: People who get a vision from God get their acts together. The vision of God shapes us. It configures us against what the world wants us to be. From that time on, we are no longer ourselves. All we are concerned about is to fulfill it. There will be a void in our lives until we fulfill it. The vision of God sets one apart from others.

It Is Inspiring: The birthing of the vision from God causes an awakening and illumination in our minds. It invigorates a new hope of a better end. It puts a significant amount of confidence that God is there with us.

It Provokes A Change: Makers and changers of history, society, system has been people with a burning vision from God. It places a level of dissatisfaction on our present state as we clamor for the new place the vision is taking us to.

It Is People-Oriented: Whatever vision God gives us, it must be for the service of humanity and the pleasure of God. It is about adding value to people's lives. This is what differentiates a vision from a profession. Professionalism and business make us concerned more about profit than the quality of life or value we provide. Some pastors and churches are mere business centers. No wonder their primary concern is the money that comes in, the type of cars of their members, the choice and location of their physical structures, the list continues. The genuine concern of the members' spiritual, physical, and mental growth is the least important to them.

Analyzing The Vision

> *"I will stand my watch and set myself on the rampart and watch to see what He will say to me and what I will answer when I am corrected. Then, the Lord answered me and said: write the vision and make it plain on tablets, that he may run who reads it. For the vision is yet for an appointed time, but at the end, it will speak, and it will not lie. Though it tarries, wait for it; because it will surely come, it will not tarry" (Habakkuk 2:1-3, NKJV).*

> *"I will climb my watchtower now and wait to see what answer God will give to my complaint. And the Lord said to me, "write my answer on a billboard, large and clear so that anyone can read at a glance and rush to tell others. But these things I plan won't happen right away. Slowly, steadily, surely, the time approaches when the vision will be fulfilled. If it seems slow, do not despair, for these things will surely come to pass. Just be patient! They will not be overdue a single day!" Habakkuk 2:1-3, TLB).*

We need to analyze a vision adequately to fulfill it. Several people receive a vision and immediately run with it without analyzing it from God's perspective. In the versions of the scripture above, we will elicit some processes in analyzing a God-given vision. They are thus:

Understanding The Vision: You need first to understand the scope and direction of the vision. God speaks from His realm. You need to bring it to our realm for better understanding.

Interpreting The Vision: Sometimes, visions come in coded forms. An example is God's vision to the Pharaoh of Egypt about the seven years of famine and years of plenty in Genesis Chapter 41. Joseph needed to explain and interpret the vision before the vision was executed. Daniel had to interpret the vision God gave to King Nebuchadnezzar in a dream in Daniel Chapter 2. Without interpretation of a vision, it will be challenging to comprehend and articulate for people to follow and execute.

Authenticating The Vision: Any vision given by God will go through some processes. Believe it or not, it may seem as if the vision is about to die at some point. God allows this in His people's lives so that we can entirely depend on and trust in His ability and capacity to provide everything necessary to accomplish the vision. He wants to receive all the glory for everything accomplished through the vision. The scriptures above said that though the vision may seem dying or slow, you have to wait for it because it will surely come true.

Timing The Vision: Every vision given by God has a set time to start. The timing is God's and not ours. We must seek the Lord concerning the timing. We are to plan as the Lord leads us in the direction of the vision. The scripture above says it is for an appointed time. Daniel understood that the children of Israel would stay in captivity for seventy years. Getting close to the set time, he started praying for the Israelites' freedom and liberation in Daniel Chapter 9.

There are two ways to check God's timing: KRONOS and KAIROS. KRONOS has to do with the arrangement of the sequence of events in our natural calendar. In contrast, KAIROS has to do with the period of completion of a particular event, which is a prerequisite to kick-starting the next event, i.e., an event in the mind of God needs to be accomplished before another event commences. Hence, the timing of the latter is contingent upon the completion of the former.

Vision Versus Ambition

Regardless of how vision and ambition look alike, they are two entities on the same plane or parallel lines. We will expand on their meanings as we discuss their similarities and differences.

Ambition is a quest to achieve something. It is a strong desire to do something. It is the desire or determination to be successful, wealthy, educated, powerful, influential the list continues. The motivating power behind ambition is self, based on the influence of the environment or the prevailing circumstance at hand.

On the contrary, vision is the ability to do what God shows you through relationship and revelation with Him; the Holy Spirit. We have learned much about vision in our previous sections in this chapter. Now, let's examine the similarities and differences between vision and ambition to know which is needed or not.

Similarities
- Both demands actions from the bearer
- Both are inspired by something or someone
- Both get blessed with an earthly rewards
- Both can be found in any field of human endeavor

Differences

Vision	Ambition
It is divine	It is earthly
It draws sight from God	It draws sight from self
It draws people closer to God	It draws people closer to self
It gives glory to God	It gives glory to self/others
Receiving is based on revelation and relationship	Receiving is based on the mood of the receiver
It increases and made clearer with time	It stagnates and fades away with time

Vision	Ambition
Giving is based on the eternal plan of God	Giving is based on the current situation
It sees challenges as a steppingstone	It sees challenges as an obstruction

With this illustration, work can be a product of vision or an ambition irrespective of the profession. A man can ambitiously start a church for profit, learn all the skills needed for it, or even employ a resident pastor while becoming the General Overseer. That church can grow as he deploys his business acumen or with some diabolical powers, but definitely, it is not from God and cannot receive God's approval.

In the same vein, an ambitious man desiring to accumulate wealth without asking for God's plan for his life can start a business venture. With his business knowledge, social capital, and financial support from friends, families and other external sources, can be successful but at the same time not receive God's approval.

I want us to know that God is interested in the redemption of the whole earth and not just humans.

> *"For it pleased the Father that in Him all the fullness should dwell, and by Him to reconcile all things to Himself, by Him, whether things on earth or things in heaven, having made peace through the blood of His cross" (Colossians 1:19-20).*

He created everyone for a specific assignment to give Him glory and bless humanity and the universe. Every vision, call, or idea we receive from God is an instruction within the broader project of redeeming the earth and its resources.

Vision Versus Burden

A burden is almost like a vision, as both have some similarities. Their source is both from God. They are both beneficial to God and man. We need to know their differences so we know when to apply them.

Vision	Burden
It reveals solutions	It reveals needs
It is taken to the people	It is taken to God
It gives birth to mission	It gives birth to vision
It increases with time	It terminates with time
It causes you to act wisely	It causes you to pray ceaselessly
The key to vision is a relationship	The key to a burden is perceived need

God can create a burden in the heart of someone to meet a particular need at a given time, but after that, it vanishes. So, God expects you to move to the next level in Him after lifting the burden. If not, whatever you do henceforth, is mechanical and devoid of God's presence and approval. Unfortunately, some people receive a burden from the Lord, and they build a tabernacle around it. We must not substitute burden for vision. Burden disappears when the need is accomplished.

Vision transcends burden and grows with time. It is God's whole agenda over a life, a family, a people's group, an organization, a nation, or even generations unborn. Vision is revealed per time until it is fully unfolded. Vision is from God handed over to man for execution. Having received a vision from God, there is a need to persuade our aged long-abused and unrenewed mind to embrace it. Never substitute vision for burden. Vision grows with time until we fully accomplish it.

God created the burning bush in Sinai to get Moses' attention to hear Him, but after that interface, we never heard about the burning bush again, even when the Israelites passed through there afterward. To this day, there has not been any burning bush experience.

A CALL FOR PRAYER
- *Using Eph1:16-19, ask God for wisdom and revelation in the knowledge of Him that your heart will be flooded with light to see only what He wants you to see.*
- *Ask God to anoint your eyes, ears, and heart, which are the instruments of you receiving His vision.*
- *Ask God for strength and capacity on the inside to do His will on the earth.*

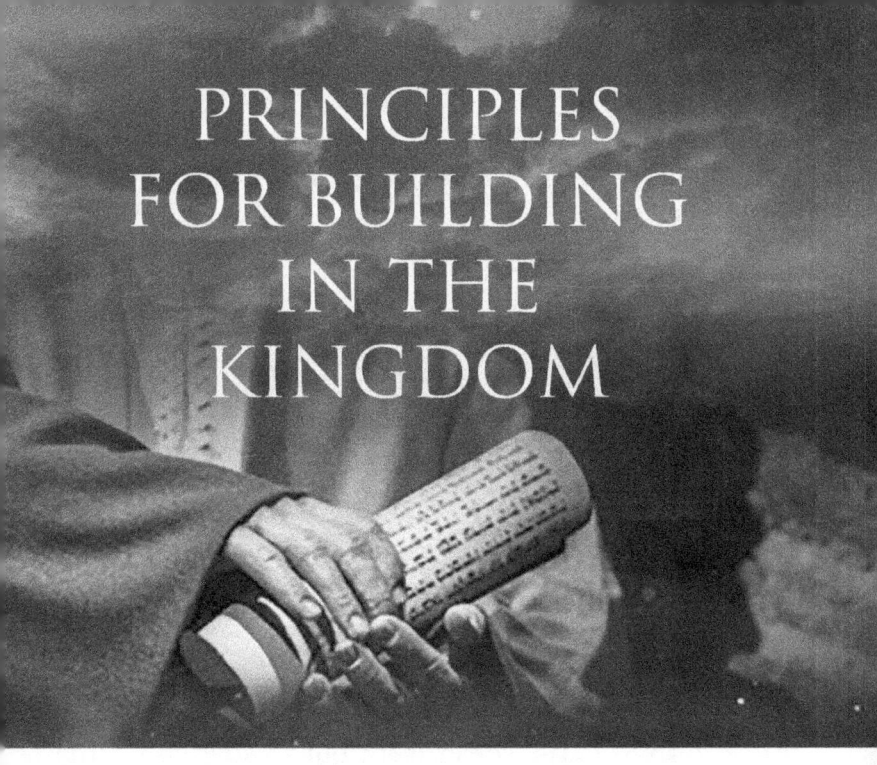

PRINCIPLES FOR BUILDING IN THE KINGDOM

CHAPTER 3

Building Principle Two: Persuasion

"And these all died in faith, not having received the promise, but having seen them afar off, and were persuaded of them, and embraced them and confessed that they were strangers and pilgrims on the earth" (Heb 11:13).

The second principle in our journey to building what is accurate and long-lasting in the sight of God is persuasion. We need to be persuaded by the vision we have received, as explained in the previous chapter. It is possible to receive a vision from the Lord and not be persuaded by it. Simply put, if we are not persuaded, then the vision is not convincing enough.

The Spirit of God gives vision into our human spirit, but our mind needs to develop to understand it for the vision to work for us on earth. Our mind is the outlet of the spirit to the physical world. Therefore, it plays a crucial role in translating a vision into physical realities.

This can be likened to the story of the Parable of the Sower in Matt 13:3-9. The sower went out to sow, and some of the seeds sown fell on rocky soil. However, the seed was planted but could not grow to its full potential due to the scorching sun. The effect is that the seed dried and withered away. It was not because it was a bad seed but because the prevailing circumstances did not allow it to grow. There was no inner substance to sustain the seed; as a result, it died. The state of our mind can abort the vision God gave us.

In that same manner, a God-given vision can suffocate and eventually fizzle out in the hand of a man who is not entirely persuaded by the vision. It does not mean the vision is not from God, but there was no collaboration between man and God.

Heb 4:1-3 says;

"Although God's promise still stands-his promise that all may enter his place of rest-we ought to tremble with fear because some of you may be on the verge of failing to get there after all. For this wonderful news-the message that God wants to save us-has been given to us just as it was to those who lived in the time of Moses. But it didn't do them any good because they didn't believe it. They didn't mix it with faith. For only we who believe God can enter into his place of rest. He has said, "I have sworn in my anger that those who don't, believe me, will never get in," even though he has been ready and waiting for them since the world began" TLB.

For the word of God to have fruitful work in our lives, we must first commit it in our mind and then believe it in our heart as the word of God.

"For this reason, we also thank God without ceasing, because when you received the word of God which you heard from us, <u>you welcomed it not as the word of men, but as it is in truth, the word of God, which also effectively works in you who believe</u>" (1 Thessalonian 2:13, NKJV).

The word of God these brethren in Thessalonica heard fully persuaded them. As a result, it worked effectively in their lives, unlike the Israelites that left Egypt with Moses.

The Israelites could not get to the Promised Land because they found it difficult to persuade their minds to believe what God said to them. It wasn't because God did not promise them, or He could not carry them through. They knew God sent Moses to deliver them, but they couldn't come to terms with their senses that 430 years of slavery suddenly came to an end. They told Moses they preferred slavery, provided they could eat garlic and cucumber instead of coming to the wilderness to suffer.

Unfortunately, some believers have received exceptional visions, dreams, and ideas from the Lord, but they locked the vision out of their lives because of the disposition of their minds. God swore to the children of Israel that those who doubted in their minds would not enter into His rest even though it has been prepared for them from the foundation of the world.

> *But what did the scriptures say concerning our father Abraham 'As it is written, I have made thee the father of many nations, before whom he believed, even God, who quickeneth the dead and calleth those things which be not as though they were. Who against hope believe in hope that he might become the father of many nations, according to that which was spoken, so shall thy seed be. And being not weak in the faith, he considered not his own body now dead, when he was about hundred years old, neither the deadness of Sarah's womb. He staggered not at the promise of God through unbelief; but was strong in faith, giving glory to God, and being fully persuaded that, what he had promised, he was able also to perform' Rom 4:17-21 (KJV).*

Taking Father Abraham as an example, the above-quoted scripture will analyze persuasion issues in the following sub-headings below.

The Power Of Persuasion
Before dealing with the power of persuasion, let us see and analyze the English dictionary meaning of persuasion.

Persuasion is the act of persuading someone to do something or believe something, a particular set of beliefs, especially about religion or politics. It is to influence someone to do something by giving him a good reason, making someone believe that something is true. It is to <u>convince by reasoning</u>.

From this definition, it is evident that persuasion is of the mind. We need to convince our minds to accept the information our spirit is receiving from the Spirit of the Lord. This is a significant mental shift we must make.

For clarity, here is a process of the flow of information from God to humans. The Spirit of God incubates our re-created human spirit, which is already in alignment with God's Spirit, enabling us to receive streams of information from God's realm and then pass it to the mind to interpret to our human world. The various compartments in our mind need to work in harmony for that word in the spirit realm to manifest in the physical realm. These, we will discuss in detail in the next subheading.

The mind needs to be convinced (persuaded) of the word coming from the spirit realm for that word to manifest in the mental and physical world. The power of persuasion of the mind is compelling and essential. **The mind can shut down the expression of what is in the spirit**. No argument; the spirit is more potent than the mind. The spirit can exist alone without the mind in its world (spirit world). However, if the spirit must manifest to the mental or physical world, the mind is the entry route through which it can happen.

Significant numbers of people who have done wonders on earth from the spirit have worked on their minds not to resist what the Spirit is saying. No wonder Apostle Paul kept admonishing the Church in Rom 12:1-3 that,

> *"We should present our bodies a living sacrifice, holy and acceptable into God and we should not be conformed to this world in our mind but be transformed by the renewing of our mind, so we can prove (verify) that which is good, acceptable and perfect will of God."*

He understands the power of the mind, so he continually draws our attention to renewing our mind so that the spirit can have free flow in the earth.

The primary reason many who have a breakthrough in the spirit but does not get to the physical is the issues of the mind. A man who has medical knowledge (mind) and then is infected with HIV/AIDS may find it difficult to believe God's divine healing because medical science says there is no cure for the virus at the moment.

There is the need to persuade the mind to believe that God's word can produce what science can't. There is an event that occurred in Acts chapter 12. Peter was put in jail by Herod, ready to be killed after the festival, but the Church went into ceaseless prayers on his behalf that God should deliver him. God answered their prayers by setting him free in a miraculous way, but that same Church praying for him could not believe his sudden deliverance. They called the girl that broke the news of his freedom mad for thinking that such could happen. Though they were laboring in the spirit, their minds never believed what they were doing.

> *"...Peter, therefore, was kept in prison: but prayer was made without ceasing of the Church unto God for him... And as Peter knocked at the door of the gate, a damsel came to hearken, named Rhoda. And when she knew Peter's voice, she opened not the gate for gladness, and ran in, and told how Peter stood before the gate. And they said to her, Thou art mad, but she constantly affirmed that it was so. Then said they, it is his angel" (Acts12:5, 13-15).*

It took God's divine intervention and few believers there, such as the girl Rhoda, for Peter's miracle to come to physical manifestation. So many of us believers are like that. This is one reason why there are few physical results despite all the spiritual activities we engage in.

What produced the miraculous for our father, Abraham, in our primary scriptures above? It was a fact that his body (his sexual life) was biologically dead because of age, but he argued with his mind that God could revitalize him by His word. He declared: "I know the fact which is, my sexual life is dead, and Sarah's womb is also dead, which means the surrounding circumstance of my life is practically impossible for me to bear a child, but the truth I have chosen to trust more is the promise of God which is higher."

This whole drama did not take place in a split second. It took time before he could get his mind to align with the word (promises) of God. The only thing that will continuously help us put the mind under control so that the spirit will flow unhindered is to transform our minds with God's word. The miracles and visions God gave to many of us have remained elusive because we neglected the importance of this part of our lives - the mind.

The Mind And Its Component

The mind is the part of us that gives us the consciousness of ourselves and the rest of the world. It is the seat of intelligence leading us into the mental and physical world. Without the corporation of the mind, we cannot live a meaningful life on earth. It is the part of us that houses the emotions, the subconscious, and the conscious. It is the outlet of the spirit.

Whatever is in the spirit, either good or bad, is given expression to the outer world through the mind. It is so strategic and indispensable that men who have traversed the spirit realm and accomplished significant feats on earth have been people who knew how to control their minds. They don't underplay what the mind can do.

Both positive and negative innovations come from the spirit realm, but the human mind interprets what we understand on earth. A man can be mighty in the spirit but produces less work on earth because of the distortion of the mind. A man cannot grow above his knowledge which is in his mind. This is why the scriptures say in Prov23:7 that as a man thinks in his heart, so he is.

The mind contains the brain, which is the seat of all intelligence, and the brain controls our nervous system, which gives sensation to the entire body. The nervous system produces the five physical senses through which we interface with the external physical world. Those senses are the sense of sight- the eyes, the sense of smell- the nose, the sense of hearing- the ear, the sense of touch- the skin, and the sense of taste-the tongue. They are called the sense organs of the body. The occultists know the importance of these organs to their activities in the spirit realm. So, they don't joke about their usage. The word of God equally charges us to train our senses to understand and obey the word of God.

See what the Bible says in Amplified version of Hebrews Chapter 5:13-14,

> *"for everyone who continues to feed on milk is obviously inexperienced and unskilled in the doctrine of righteousness (of conformity to the divine will in purpose, thought, and action), for he is a mere infant [not able to talk yet]! But solid food is for full-grown men, for those whose senses and mental faculties are trained by practice to discriminate and distinguish between what is morally good and noble and what is evil and contrary either to divine or human law."*

In other words, your maturity in the things of God is determined by the amount of training your sense organs have been subjected to in understanding what the word of God says. Such a person no longer judges things based on his external influences without first subjecting it to the scrutiny of God's Word to know the mind of God towards that thing. When this is done repeatedly over time, that person develops the mind of Christ, which is one of the significant signs of maturity in Christ.

The sense organs are the gateways between our human spirit and our mind. We use the sense organs to gather information which eventually affects the way our spirit operates. Those who expose their minds to pornography all the time will ultimately start practicing it. No wonder God warns us in the book of Proverbs to always guard our heart diligently (mind) with the word of God, for out of it comes the issues of life, whether good or bad. These sense organs are the portals through which we receive information that shapes our human spirit.

The mind is a reservoir of information of yesteryears of our personal and other people's experiences, philosophies, and values we believe and live with over the years. Some information is transferred from one generation to the other without any formal teaching through the mind. Newborn babies automatically know what to do with their mother's breast without any formal training. This was one reason God accounted the world to be sinners even if you are a newborn baby. It was because of one man's sin – the first man on earth through which the human race came. The knowledge of his sinful nature entered every human being, so they all sinned in the eyes of God.

The information we consume every day shapes who we are. They determine whether we are high or low, rich or poor, strong or weak, a leader or a follower. Ultimately, they determine what we become and how far we can go in the things of life. Motivational speakers say, "if you can see it, you can get it." Though this is a fact, there are processes to accomplish it. God intends to remove all those thoughts we got right from Adam till now that have not allowed us to grow and become great in Him.

When one gets born-again, God recreates his spirit anew. His mind remains the same with all the deposits it has accumulated over the years. These deposits include all we have exposed our sense organs to from cradle and imbibed over the years. Now, we will gradually start debugging every knowledge that opposes the word of God in our lives. The more we debug and replacing them with God's word and values, the better and more mature Christians we become in God. John the Baptist said that he would decrease so that He (Jesus' values) might increase in him.

The type and amount of information we carry in our minds has a significant effect in shaping our spiritual life, which in totality affects our fullness in life.

The Mind: The Seat of all Battles

There are two parallel forces on earth that will never meet. They determine what we do, what we say, our decisions and ultimately influence our actions. Paul's struggle with these forces when growing up in God is evident in the scripture.

> *"We know that the Law is spiritual, but I am a creature of the flesh [carnal, unspiritual], having been sold into slavery under [the control of] sin, for I do not understand my own actions [I am baffled, bewildered]. I do not practice or accomplish what I wish, but I do the very thing that I loathe [which my moral instinct condemns]. Now, if I do [habitually] what is contrary to my desire, [that means that] I acknowledge and*

agree that the Law is good (morally excellent) and that I take sides with it. However, it is no longer I who do the deed, but the sin [principle] which is at home in me and has possession of me. For I know that nothing good dwells within me, that is, in my flesh. I can will what is right, but I cannot perform it. [I have the intention and urge to do what is right, but no power to carry it out.] For I fail to practice the good deeds, I desire to do, but the evil deeds that I do not desire to do are what I am [ever] doing. Now, if I do what I do not desire to do, it is no longer I doing it [it is not myself that acts], but the sin [principle] which dwells within me [fixed and operating in my soul]. So I find it to be a law (rule of action of my being) that when I want to do what is right and good, evil is ever-present with me, and I am subject to its insistent demands. For I endorse and delight in the Law of God in my inmost self [with my new nature]. But I discern in my bodily members [in the sensitive appetites and wills of the flesh] a different law (rule of action) at war against the law of my mind (my reason) and making me a prisoner to the law of sin that dwells in my bodily organs [in the sensitive appetites and wills of the flesh]. O unhappy and pitiable and wretched man that I am! Who will release and deliver me from [the shackles of] this body of death? Oh, thank God! [He will!] through Jesus Christ (the Anointed One) our Lord! So then indeed I, of myself with the mind and heart, serve the Law of God, but with the flesh the law of sin" (Rom 7:14-25, AMP).

From the above scripture, there are two areas of conflict where the man becomes helpless. The entire human race is tied to these two forces. Whatever you do, act, or build, you are either yielding to one or the other. It has nothing to do with religion or whatever you believe or practice. It has to do with life. So long as you have life, you must either obey one or the other. The two areas are the law of the flesh and the law of the spirit. Another version of the scripture calls it the **lower nature** and the **higher nature**. It is called nature because it is within us, proceeding out of us.

There is a battle of who controls the man: the flesh or the spirit. The mind expresses these two forces and struggles with whose dictate to follow. In this context, the flesh is the outer body and the spiritual, Adamic nature in the soul where we have the mind. This flesh determines the value system, the philosophies, the Babylonian mindset, and all of its anti-God operations.

The flesh resists God from expressing Himself in us and the world. It is the unregenerate mind of man inherited from the first Adam. In that same vein, the spirit is also spiritual but subject to the dictates of God. It is the regenerated part of man that yields to God.

The illustration is this: As unbelievers, the flesh controls our actions when we don't know God. Our spirit is dead, and the Spirit of God cannot influence our actions. When we give our lives to Christ (believers), our spirit is renewed, and our mind starts receiving illumination through the word of God we receive, and hence, the Adamic (lower nature) starts to give way to the nature of God.

The more of God's word we imbibe, the more our mind is also changed, and our sense organs enable us to filter what goes in and out of us using God's word as the metric. The more our judgments on what we hear about what God wants us to do, become more apparent. Therefore, the mind becomes the major battlefield on whether we will fulfill the word of God given to us or not.

Bringing the Mind into Obedience

My beloved, I want to start by saying that the mind cannot be born again, just as our spirit does. It will never be. Always, we must keep drawing our minds to obey the word of God. As explained previously, the two forces on earth still fight to take over our minds for their purposes. Our prayers on their own cannot change the posture of our minds; they can only strengthen us in carrying it out. We have total responsibility for changing our minds with God's word, and our willingness to do so is necessary.

The scripture we know too well that explains this is in Rom 12:1-2which says that we (believers), not God, should present our bodies and renew our minds. Sometimes, we take days praying and fasting for some of our values systems to change without participating in that change. How do you think it will work? Where it does work, it is not our prayers but out of God's magnanimity and favor. It does not mean our prayers are not needed; they are, but our effort counts more since it is even more of God's desire that we change.

It takes great effort from us for our minds to become submissive to the word of God. It takes our constant discipline of self to obey. We have to be discreet in what we expose our sense organs to receive. The system of Babylon will always want to prevail, but we have to resist it vehemently. It also takes our constant study of the scriptures to understand the mind of God. The importance of this cannot be over-emphasized.

Unbelief: The Blockage Of Miracle

> *"Therefore, since a promise remains of entering His rest, let us fear lest any of you seem to have come short of it. For indeed the gospel was preached to us as well as to them, but the word which they heard did not profit them, not being mixed with faith in those who heard it" (Heb 4:1-2, NKJV).*

All the Israelites who doubted God and wandered in the wilderness died without receiving the promise. Only Caleb and Joshua eventually made it to the promised land because they fixed their minds on God's word and acted on it. Even after experiencing significant manifestations of God's power, the Israelites missed out on God's best for them because of their mindset.

Our mind (soul) is potent and must not be taken for granted. It gives room to our self-will and is the central destructive element in our ability to enter God's rest. Self-awareness and not God-awareness is our greatest misery and enemy to God the Father. Our self-righteousness and self-exploration are anti-God. God wants to lead, but then we feel we can achieve much by our intellect, but eventually, we lose everything and become foolish in our thoughts.

There are two significant trees in the Garden of Eden: the tree of life and the tree of the knowledge of good and evil. Eating from the tree of life draws us to God's life in the Spirit, by faith. Eating from the tree of the knowledge of good and evil draws us to the soul's life by our perception, intelligence, and worldview.

> *"Blessed are those who do His commandments, that they may have right to the tree of life and may enter through the gates into the city" (Rev 22:14).*

We cannot please God or work in the revealed plan of God if we succumb to the unregenerate soul. It will always thwart God's purpose on earth. The soul must be renewed and persuaded to follow God's plan.

Western culture has taught us to depend on our intellect. Education is regarded as the answer to humanity's social ills. The basic theory seems to be that we will become smart enough to rule our lives successfully if we have adequate knowledge. Independence is essential to our way of thinking. If we are intellectually sharp enough and have enough money, we can do what we want and have what we want. Indeed, we think this will produce peace and happiness. This is partaking of the tree of knowledge of good and evil. It was what took Adam and Eve out of the garden.

The enemy lured them to focus on themselves and no longer on God, so they fell. Years after, humanity is still following the same steps. Yes, education and mental skills are essential aspects of life; but they alone cannot take us to God and His planned destiny for our lives. It will not lead us to that abundant life. We should get an education and mental skills with the mind of using it to access God's revealed instructions in our given purpose in life. God's revealed truth should guides what and how we expose our mind and not vice versa.

Case Study Of This Principle

We draw an inference from the episode between our Lord Jesus Christ and Peter when God was about to open the door of salvation to the non-Jews (Gentiles). He orchestrated a drama which Peter, in his logical mind, refused to accept.

> *"At Caesarea, there was a man named Cornelius, a centurion in what was known as the Italian Regiment. He and all his family were devout and God-fearing; he gave generously to those in need and prayed to God regularly. One day at about three in the afternoon, he had a vision.*

He distinctly saw an angel of God, who came to him and said, "Cornelius!" Cornelius stared at him in fear. "What is it, Lord?" he asked. The angel answered, "Your prayers and gifts to the poor have come up as a memorial offering before God. Now send men to Joppa to bring back a man named Simon, who is called Peter. He is staying with Simon the tanner, whose house is by the sea." When the angel who spoke to him had gone, Cornelius called two of his servants and a devout soldier who was one of his attendants. He told them everything that had happened and sent them to Joppa. About noon the following day, as they were on their journey and approaching the city, Peter went up on the roof to pray. He became hungry and wanted something to eat, and while the meal was being prepared, he fell into a trance. He saw heaven opened and something like a large sheet being let down to earth by its four corners. It contained all kinds of four-footed animals, as well as reptiles of the earth and birds of the air. Then a voice told him, "Get up, Peter. Kill and eat." "Surely not, Lord!" Peter replied. "I have never eaten anything impure or unclean." The voice spoke to him a second time, "Do not call anything impure that God has made clean." This happened three times, and immediately the sheet was taken back to heaven. While Peter was wondering about the meaning of the vision, the men sent by Cornelius found out where Simon's house was and stopped at the gate. They called out, asking if Simon, who was known as Peter, was staying there. While Peter was still thinking about the vision, the Spirit said to him, "Simon, three men are looking for you. So get up and go downstairs. Do not hesitate to go with them, for I have sent them" (Acts 10:1-20 NIV).

According to tradition and culture, the Jews do not eat those animals, but God used that experience to point Peter in a new direction about His salvation plan to the entire human race. Peter could not reason it out in his mind even though he knew it was the Lord speaking to him. His earth-bound mind could not resonate with what God was saying. Peter's logical mind could have stopped the miracle if not for divine intervention. The whole episode did not align with his mindset, so he rejected it. It took God's intervention for that miracle to take place.

A CALL FOR PRAYER

- *Ask the Lord for strength and capacity to accommodate His speakings in your life.*

- *Ask for the proper alignment of your spirit, soul, and body in obedience to the word of God.*

- *Speak to your mind to be submissive to the dictates of your spirit, at all times.*

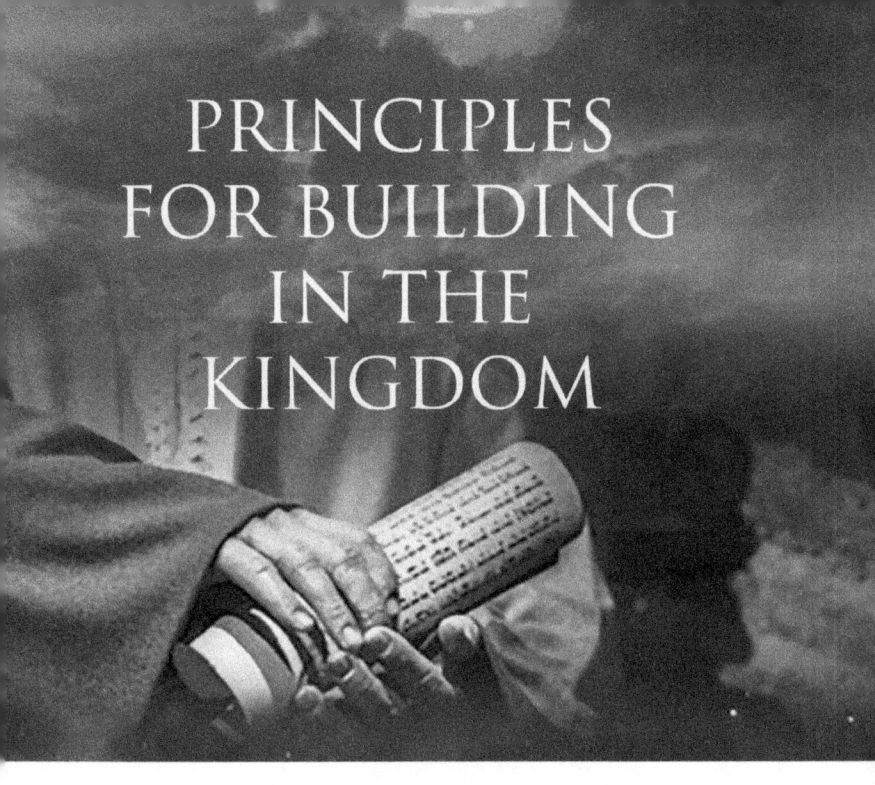

PRINCIPLES FOR BUILDING IN THE KINGDOM

CHAPTER 4

Building Principle Three: Embrace

"And these all died in faith, not having received the promise, but having seen them afar off, and were persuaded of them, and embraced them and confessed that they were strangers and pilgrims on the earth" Heb 11:13.

The third principle in our journey to building what is accurate and long-lasting in the sight of God is embracing. We should embrace the vision or purpose God has given to us. It is not enough to receive the vision or be convinced and persuaded of its authenticity. Besides, it is required to move forward and embrace it in our lives.

To embrace a word or an idea is different from being persuaded of it. However, I will not embrace everything that persuades me. If an idea or vision from God persuades me, my mind must believe in God's power to accomplish it. Nevertheless, it is not every idea or vision I will embark on, even though I believe it will work.

The word 'embrace' speaks of two things or people coming together in their affection for each other to willingly become one (inseparable) on acceptance of the idea or vision; two entities fusing willingly.

In chemical science, two elements come together to form either a mixture or a compound. The joining or union talked about in this chapter is that of a compound.

A mixture is the combination of two or more substances combined but not chemically bonded. Those substances can return to their original form; hence their union is not permanent. The elements are only physically joined and not by chemical means. An example is mixing sand and water. They still retain their original form.

Building Principle Three: Embrace

A compound is the combination of two substances under a chemical bond. The new substance formed cannot be broken apart from the original substances again. It takes the shape, nature, and character of the new substance. An example is the combination of hydrogen and oxygen to form water ($2H2+022 \rightarrow H2O$). This chemical process of forming a compound is how the word 'embrace' works when God's vision fuses with a man's life. They become inseparable and difficult to alter.

In Christianity, this is called an 'encounter.' The man never remains the same again. When this happens, the man's life automatically changes; his appetite, values, operating system, and lifestyle change. This process works in every aspect of our lives, including the five-fold ministry, business, politics, and career. The Holy Spirit is that catalyst that stirs up the chemical reaction for the fusion.

The Mystery of Two Becoming One

"And said, For this cause shall a man leave father and mother and shall cleave to his wife: and they twin shall be one flesh…" (Matt 19:5).

"For no man ever yet hated his own flesh, but nourisheth and cherisheth it, even as the Lord the Church: for we are members of his body, of his flesh and of his bones. For this, cause shall a man leave his father and mother and shall be joined into his wife, and they two shall be one flesh. This is a great mystery: but I speak concerning Christ and the church" (Eph 5:29-32).

The Bible sees this union as a great mystery. In the scriptures above, two coming together to become one negates scientific calculations. It is the mystery behind Jesus' union with the Church to become one whole body. The technology behind this process is, in these words: leaving, cleaving, and becoming one flesh.

Process Flow To Embrace God's Vision

Leaving: Leaving is the first stage in the process of embracing the vision or ideas from God. We have to leave our past lives, experiences, successes, failures, knowledge, and all we have accumulated, focusing, and pursuing what God will ever say to us now. We must be responsive to God and know when He is changing direction, and follow Him wholeheartedly. Imagine if Abraham was unwilling to leave his father (Terah) and his people; the nation of Israel whom God loves may not have been birthed. If we do not leave our past achievements and experiences, whether good or bad, we cannot grasp and cleave to the new things God is doing or saying to us.

One of the major hindrances to embracing God's plans and purpose this end time is our past experiences, achievements, and the societal norms we have imbibed. In Gen 19:1-26, Lot's wife could not embrace God's new things in her time because of wrong desires, lust for wealth, and past achievements. Even though she was persuaded that God was about to do a new thing in Sodom, she could not embrace it. She looked back. Looking back signifies that she couldn't fuse herself with the Word of God even when she knew that God was leading them.

The children of Israel could not enter the Promised Land that flows with milk and honey because they failed to embrace the reality of seeing themselves in a land where they would not struggle too much to meet their needs as they did in Egypt. Though God gave them the vision of the land, yet they did not believe in His power to lead them there. They couldn't migrate in their mind. They were speaking migration with their mouth, but their hearts were saying something different – "we are all right with our sufferings in Egypt. We can cope with it."

The first process in embracing what God is saying is to develop the mentality of a sojourner – the ability to leave all that you know and follow a new course in God.

Cleaving: Cleaving is the second stage in the process of embracing the vision or ideas from God. Cleaving means to come or be in close contact with; stick or hold together and resist separation. In achieving God's purpose for our lives, after we have left the things that can weigh us down and prevent us from pursuing the plans of God, we are to seek and cleave to those things that will activate those words in our lives. If we 'leave' without 'cleaving,' our journey will be truncated along the way. There are specific values, habits, and lifestyles we need to stick into our lives to finish well.

Apart from the standard kingdom value system, we should take up some specific training and acquire skills and education related to the particular pathway God has called us into. Following God's vision for our lives would ultimately shape who we become for the rest of our lives. Our lives henceforth take the design and shape of the destiny God has ordained for us. I would want us to note something here that God's purpose for our lives determines the type of skill, education, or training we undergo and not vice versa.

When you discover God's purpose for your life, you build structures around that purpose. Our generation finds it challenging to track God's destiny over our lives because of the things we have encumbered ourselves with. We want to acquire and achieve much before we come to ask His will for our lives. We want to force God's hands to approve our work simply because it is good and lovely in our eyes. We feel that walking in God's purpose for our lives is different from our day-to-day routine work. I am concerned that is not right. Our whole life should center on God's purpose.

We are required to learn and seek God's will for our individual lives. After diligently doing that, we should have honest discussions with some senior people to plan the way forward on how to execute the plan to profit to God, ourselves, the Body of Christ, and the entire earth. This must be people vetted by all standards of the scriptures with proven Christian character.

God spoke to Joshua in Josh 1:8 that;

> *"This book of the law should not depart from his mouth but to meditate upon it day and night for out of it lies his prosperity and success."*

This book refers not to the whole Bible as no one can meditate on the entire Bible daily. This book mentioned has to do with that specific purpose He designed for you out of His full purpose (contained in the Bible). You are to guard it with your life because your life in God depends on it. Joshua chapter 1:8 was a charge from Moses to Joshua before his departure. He called that book of the law 'your very life.' Understanding that book of the law determines the scope of education, experience, the skill you need to acquire. Your whole life should cleave to this law of God crafted specifically for you.

One Flesh: The last stage in the process of embracing is becoming one flesh. You have to leave your past and all the things that will not allow you to move forward in the purpose of God for your life. After that, you then cleave to the kingdom's values, lifestyles, and cultures that will enhance God's purpose for your life. Lastly, you have to marry those values and visions from God. The pathway to its fulfillment which God gave, now becomes your pathway. You now become a co-owner of the purpose, like a man and a woman coming together in marriage to become one flesh. At this point, no more individual or personal purpose; instead, the purpose of the man becomes the purpose of the woman. You no longer quote the scripture as a reported speech (what someone wrote and told you is correct); instead, you speak with great confidence and assurance as if you were there when it was written or you wrote it.

When you speak, nobody can recognize the difference between your life and the words you heard from God. You can die for the sake of that cause (purpose); that is, you can go to any length for the Word to fulfill in your life. When they were hungry, Jesus declared to His people, saying, *"My meat (food) is to do the works of Him that sent me and to finish it."* The Bible, trying to describe the passion and zeal with which Jesus carried out His Father's purpose, told us how He (Jesus) made a whip to flog people who were selling in the temple. He was ready to face whatever consequences the people might bring as a result of His action. The purpose of God and His life have become one, so He no longer derives joy and satisfaction outside of that purpose.

Hebrews chapter 11 is full of people who in their days did extraordinary things for God. They esteemed God's purpose in their lives more important than their own lives, their families, and whatever anybody can aspire to become in this world. Abraham offered to sacrifice (killed) his one and only son in his old age, not minding the consequences because of God's purpose. The three Hebrew children offered to sacrifice their lives because of what they believed, even when it seemed that God wasn't ready to defend them.

> **Until your passion for the purpose of God in your life becomes an obsession, you are not yet one flesh with that purpose**

God seeks men and women who agree to partner with His divine agenda for humanity and become one flesh with His purpose. These are people whose lives mean nothing to them and are willing to step up and face challenges when God's agenda is at stake.

By the Spirit of God, the earth will soon witness myriads of believers in diverse fields of human endeavor whose allegiance is only to their King (Jesus) and His kingdom.

THE COURAGE NEEDED FOR THE EMBRACE

The Man And His Purpose Of Creation
Right from creation, humanity has always been associated

with purpose. Our lives make no sense without a purpose. Though this purpose may be self-given, God-given, or even society influenced. It may be legitimate or illegitimate, good or bad. Whatever the purpose, it is intrinsic to our lives. There is a saying that "if you don't live for something, you die for nothing." Every human being on earth lives for something. It depends on what that thing is. Not living for something (purposeless life) is still a purpose in the person's eyes living it.

If you think you have a purpose that may benefit many people does not automatically make it God's purpose. Yes, we have the brain to develop fantastic ideas that turn out to be excellent as far as humans are concerned. However, it can be self-induced or society influenced. We must allow God to breathe into us and give us His vision, which becomes our purpose for living.

A scripture in Psam104:21-30 says that the young lion waits for God for his food irrespective of his strength and power to fend for himself. Another scripture in Job 32:8 says that there is a spirit in man, but the Almighty's inspiration provides him light and understanding. This light and understanding can only come by the Almighty God's inspiration, not by our human intellect, position in society, or our maneuvering.

The point here is that we should put aside our personal, selfish, and myopic purpose to run with God's purpose for our lives and fulfill it, regardless of what significance society has attributed to us. We must come to that point in our lives when the creative purpose of God becomes our obsession. It is at that juncture that our lives are then rearranged and adjusted by the purpose of God. This purpose then becomes the turning point of our lives that we cannot do anything without it. Our values, lifestyles, and characters are then reshaped based on this revelation.

The kingdom of David is built based on the character and the lifestyle of David. His kingdom was characterized by warfare, victories, and heightened intimacy with God, as his purpose was to bring people to a higher level in God. The purpose of God in the life of a man determines his status in his generation. God's Word came to Moses to be the deliverer of the Jews from the Egyptian bondage. After receiving the Word (vision), he doubted his ability for the assignment due to his speech impairment, the difficulty of convincing his people, and the impossibility of Pharaoh letting them go. After a convincing dialogue with God, he accepted and embraced the vision. At that point, he made it personal and was ready to face whatever the consequence. He became one with God in fulfilling the purpose of bringing the Israelites out of Egypt. From then on, Moses began to see oppositions as steppingstones and not a hurdle.

The Word Becoming Flesh

"And the Word became flesh and dwelt among us, and we beheld His glory, the glory as of the only begotten of the Father, full of grace and truth" (John 1:14).

> *"That which was from the beginning which we have heard, which we have seen with our eyes, which we have looked upon, and our hands have handled, of the word of life"* (I John 1:1).

For any vision of God to prosper in us and through us, we must make the vision flesh and blood in us (part of our entire life) beyond the realm of conviction. It has to do with accepting and making it part and parcel of our daily life.

Jesus is the Word made flesh, dwelt with us, seen and handled by the Apostles. The Apostles made the invisible visible. In that premise, our ideas, visions, and purposes from God, living in the unseen realm, must translate into the seen realm.

We have so many believers who can give detail information about what God wants them to do, but ultimately, they never do them. That vision has not yet become flesh and blood in them though they talk about it. When God's purpose becomes flesh and blood in a man, he takes ownership and responsibility for it. Henceforth, he sees it as a divine assignment given to him by God.

In a particular scripture, Jesus said 'my' duty or 'my' meat is to do the works of Him that sent me and to finish it. His life's sole purpose was to do the works of Him that sent Him. (emphasis is on 'my'- personalizing the work). In essence, Jesus said that the totality of His life's endeavor is to do the works of Him that sent Him. Doing the works of the Father is what gives Him joy and satisfaction.

Remember when Jesus went into the temple of God and saw people misusing it, He did not shy away from confronting them, like most of us would do today. Instead, He took a whip and drove them out of the temple. He was able to do this because He has embraced God's purpose and made it flesh and blood in His life. His passion and commitment for the things of God were influencing His behavior at every instance.

Some of us quote scriptures as if we are afraid or do not believe them because the Word we are quoting has not been made flesh in us. We have not embraced it. Though we know it is God's Word, and God has the power to fulfill His Word, but we have not come to terms with those scriptures. There is no confidence in us when declaring the mind of God to the dying world. Most of us will capitulate if we are pressured and persecuted over the scriptures we quote, as Shadrach, Meshach, and Abednego were in the scripture. Such quotations can never produce any result as long as we continue in that way.

When a man's vision, idea, or purpose becomes flesh and blood, he ceases to be scared of failing. He will no longer see that assignment as part-time. It is common to hear believers sayings something like this: "God's work is different from my work." When you embrace the vision of God, it consumes you, eats you up, that you cannot see your work again but His work in your life. That is the type of believers God wants to unleash on earth in these last days. A people that will dare the devil just because they believe that it is their life course.

The men of David were ready to risk their very lives, which they did on several occasions for the wellbeing of their leader, David. They did not do this out of compulsion but out of a sense of duty and urgency, born out of the realization of a purpose.

Martin Luther, the reformer, dared and defied the then-ruling Pope and the Catholic Church's authority in his days. He eventually died because of his strong will towards the purpose of God for his life. Dr. Martin Luther King Jr. of America preached and died defending the truth even when he had the option to stop the pursuit of social justice and live comfortably with his family. He defied the emotional attraction of his family for God's purpose in his life.

When you embrace the vision of God, you see your duty as your cross. You don't cry and complain because others do not have the same experience as you. You don't see it as God's punishing you. In the scriptures, Joseph, going through all those tortures in the hand of his people and several others, was part of God's eternal plan for his life to fulfill God's purpose for him and his generation. His brothers sold him as a slave. When he got an opportunity amid the entire drama to retaliate, he did not. But instead, he said that God allowed it to be so, that He might be a preserver of posterity for generations yet unborn.

CASE STUDY OF THIS PRINCIPLE

Let us examine the life of Jonah in the Bible as our case study on this principle.

God sent Jonah to go to Nineveh and preach to them, for their sins have gone up to God. Jonah heard God clearly (vision) and understood the massage (persuasion) but refused to align himself with the vision (no embrace).

Jonah represents the typical believer of the 21st century. God was in continuous communication with Jonah throughout the event, just as God always communicates with His people today. God is speaking every day. Jonah did not only heard God but understood God's intent. God's intention is conveyed in His words apart from the immediate utterance. Jonah allowed his personal and corporate bias with the people of Nineveh to hinder his obedience. In the same vein, most of us hear God.

However, we subtly refuse to fuse our lives with the Word because of personal biases to the person we are sent to or the prevailing circumstances the message was intended to address. Though despite Jonah's antics, God's intent prevailed.

A CALL FOR PRAYER

- *Ask God for the capacity and insight to see His works in your life.*

- *Ask God for faith and strength to believe His words into your life despite the challenging environment fighting against this Word.*

- *Receive an enlarged heart to build according to God's pattern and principles.*

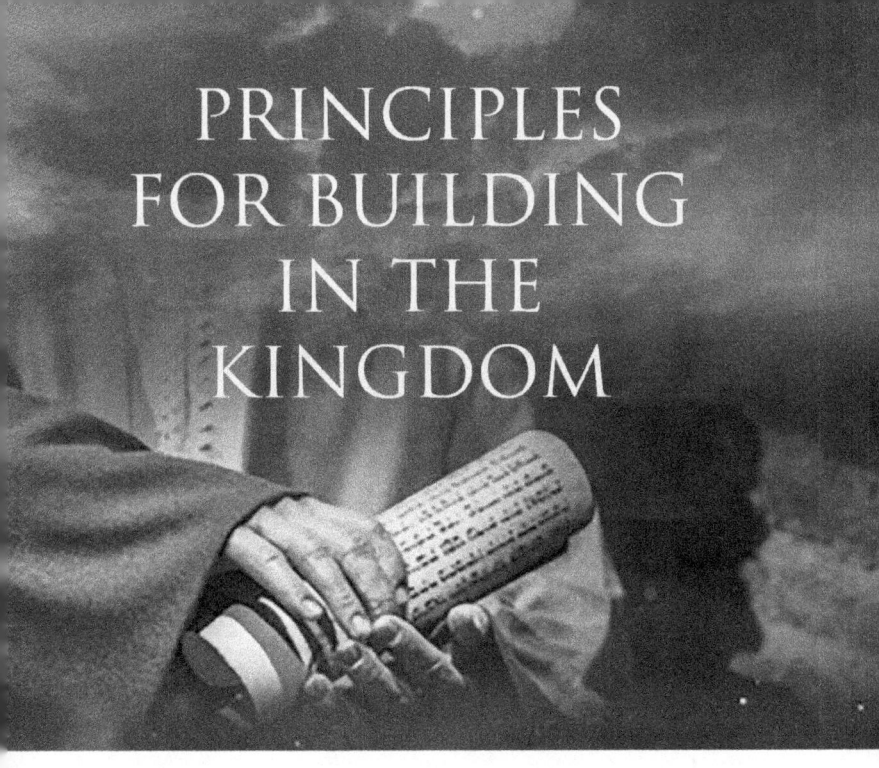

PRINCIPLES FOR BUILDING IN THE KINGDOM

CHAPTER FIVE

Building Principle Four: Confession

"These all died in faith, not having received the promises, but having seen them afar off, and were persuaded of them, and embraced them, and <u>confessed that they were strangers and pilgrims on the earth</u>" (Hebrews 11:13).

The fourth principle in our journey to building what is accurate and long-lasting in the sight of God is confession. Confession is the last stage in this building process. It is the confession of our new and revealed position that God spoke and declared to us. The first three stages or principles are activities within the individual, but this last principle is an activity you do to the external environment outside yourself. Your environment needs to know the processes of God within you. The water baptism we undergo does not make us born-again, but it is the outward show of what has taken place in the spirit so that no one will leave an excuse.

God will want us to declare to the three worlds (world of angels, the world of demons, and the world of men) that we are transformed, moving from the earthly realm to the heavenly realm.

The word 'confess' in this context has nothing to do with confessing our sins. It originated from the Greek word 'Dabar,' which means to loudly and authoritatively speak out. This speaking is not just saying whatever comes into your mouth or whatever you feel like saying. Not even what someone like your pastor or anyone else asks you to say. This speaking has to align with the processes taking place in your life over time. You must be speaking to declare the understanding of your new position and location in the spirit.

With this understanding, you speak with confidence and with authority. You do not merely mutter words or speak cowardly. You speak with such authenticity that your words convey power and authority to your audience as Jesus did in this scripture.

> *"When Jesus had finished saying these things, the crowds were astonished at His teaching, because He taught as one who had authority, and not as their scribes" (Matthew 7:28-29, BSB).*

The only word synonymous with confession in this context is declaration. It is crucial in building according to God's pattern. After God has conceived what He intends to build at the beginning of creation, He declared it by saying, "let there be," and it became. **It is the declaration of the new that nullifies the old.**

The Power Of Confession

> *"…That if you confess with your mouth the Lord Jesus and believe in your heart that God has raised Him from the dead, you will be saved. For with the heart, one believes unto righteousness, <u>and with the mouth, confession is made unto salvation</u>" (* **Rom 10:9-10).**

In analyzing Romans 10:9-10, we need to bear these in mind: to believe in God and have all the knowledge about God is good and commendable, but it is not enough. It will not guarantee our salvation unless we accompany our belief with a confession. The **Bible** says with the heart (within the person), he believes, which results unto righteousness (right standing before God), but he needs his mouth to declare openly to gain salvation from the world and his foe. He needs to declare what he has believed so that he can be set free from the entanglement of Babylon, sin, sickness, and disease. Speaking is the key to our deliverance.

Some believers feel that following God's ways (personal righteousness in Him) is all they need to excel in this life. My brothers and sisters, it is not enough as far as this earth is concerned. Do you believe that the enemy can still shoot and injure a believer with all his righteousness and perfection? Read Ps 64:1-6. The enemy randomly shoots his arrow against the righteous. Let's take a cue from the life of Job and be wise.

In His Word, the Lord Jesus said, *"Whoever confesses me in the world; him will I confess before the angels of God and my Father in heaven" Lk 12:8; Matt 10:32.*

There Are Many Things We Can Confess

We can confess our new place in God

We can confess our authority in the Lord

We can confess the Lordship of our Lord Jesus Christ

We can confess our migration to our new positions in God

We can confess our deliverance from the stronghold of Babylon

Our confessing Jesus on earth is what guarantees our salvation in the presence of the Father. In as much as confession is essential, it is needful to know what to confess. Do not confess under compulsion. Today, in our churches, we read some scriptural promises and even copy them out as books and ask our brethren to claim those promises by faith. That is not how it works. Faith needs substances (internal processes) to work. The Bible says faith without work (substance) is dead.

Our confession must be born out of the processes of God's dealings in our lives that are relevant to the scriptures. It is what you believe that you will confess. What you believe must come out of your revelational knowledge of God. That is what works. The seven sons of Sceva in Acts 19:13-16 called (confessed) Jesus without knowing Him personally by revelation. Unfortunately, the demon they were trying to cast out of the victim leaped on them, overpowered them, wounded them, tore their clothes, and chased them out of the house naked. Though they called the name of Jesus, they never understood or believed what they were doing. There was no experiential knowledge of Jesus in their lives. They had no living relationship with Him.

The depth of our knowledge and belief in Jesus must correspond with our declaration of Him. This is what determines our salvation and effectiveness as believers.

You are a believer does not mean that you are immune to Satan's attack and oppression. Two believers can be in an environment; one can withstand a satanic attack while the other can't. The reason is not that one is more righteous or holy than the other. Whoever prevails has more in-depth revelational knowledge of God, which eventually translates into his audacious declaration on earth. This guarantees our victory as believers here on earth.

Life And Death In The Power Of The Tongue

> *"A man's stomach shall be satisfied from the fruits of his mouth; from the produce of his lips, he shall be filled. Death and life are in the power of the tongue, and those who love it will eat its fruit" (Proverb 18:20-21).*

Whatever we say in the natural has consequences in the spirit. Our words can either build or destroy our destiny in God. Our words are significant in our lives. Medical science has proven that when a person says he is tired, his body's cells responsible for strength become weak, making him weak. Also, in the face of greatest weakness, when a man declares to himself that he is strong without wavering in his heart, his adrenaline rises to give him a measure of strength.

Most times, when people who have actively worked all their lives retire without finding another job to keep them active, they start dying gradually even if they are not old enough.

Again in the previous sub-heading, we saw in this scripture below that,

> "...*who sharpen their tongue like a sword, and bend their bows to shoot their arrows – <u>bitter words</u>, that they may shoot in secret at the blameless; suddenly they shoot at him and do not fear...' (Ps 64: 3 & 4).*

Human words are interchangeably used as spear and sword to shoot at people. No doubt, spoken words can affect people and reshape human destiny. Imagine how much power they will have over the spiritual realm if the words we speak in the physical have power over our body and mental realm.

Scriptures admonish us to speak what God says about us and not what the environment compels us to say. Our environment should not influence our response to the challenges of life. Our confession should come out of the revealed information God has given to us through His infallible word.

Proverb 18:20-21says that death and life are in the power (control, authority) of the tongue. The tongue determines whether you live or die. Though the tongue is a little member, it shapes the activities of the whole body. See how the Bible describes the function of the tongue in James 3:3-10. It is incredible to understand the power God committed to the tongue at creation.

> *"Indeed, we put bits in horses' mouth that they may obey us, and we turn their whole body. Look also at ships; although they are so large and are driven by fierce winds, they are turned by a very small rudder wherever that pilot desires. Even so, the tongue is a little member and boasts great things. See how great a forest a little fire kindles! And the tongue is a fire, a world of iniquity. The tongue is so set among our members that it defiles the whole body and sets on fire the course of nature, and it is set on fire by hell. For every kind of beast and bird, of reptiles and creature of the sea, is tamed and has been tamed by mankind. But no man can tame the tongue. It is an unruly evil, full of deadly poison. With it, we bless God and Father, and with it, we curse men who have been made in the similitude of God. Out of the same mouth proceed blessing and cursing."*

This scripture explains how much control the tongue has over the whole body and even the course of nature.

In this building process, what comes out of the tongue is very important. If accurately spoken, it portrays what is in our hearts. Our mouth ought to be the declaration point of what is in our hearts. If the mouth fails to speak, all the processes of God in us would be in vain.

> *"A good man brings good things out of the good stored up in his heart, and an evil man brings evil things out of the evil stored up in his heart. For the mouth speaks what the heart is full of" (Luke 6:45, NIV).*

The Wandering Israelite

> *"By faith, Abraham obeyed when he was called to go out to the place which he would receive as an inheritance. And he went out, not knowing where he was going. By faith, he dwelt in the land of promise as in a foreign country, dwelling in tent with Isaac and Jacob, the heirs with him of the same promise, for they waited for the city which has foundation, whose building and Maker is God" (Heb 11:8-10).*

This scripture was Abraham's account when God called him out of his country to go where he never knew. He had no glimmer of how the place looks before he obeyed. God gave him a glimpse of how and what the place looks like – The Lord said to Abram,

> *"Leave your land, your relatives, and your Father's home. Go to the land that I will show you. I will make you a great nation. I will bless you. I will make your name great, and you will be a blessing. I will bless those who bless you, and whoever curses you, I will curse. Through you, every family on earth will be blessed" (Gen 12:1-3, GWT).*

God promised Abraham a land that flows with milk and honey, a promise of eternal blessing that all the families of the earth shall be blessed through him. This promise never came through until after 430 years, when the Israelites got to the Promised Land.

> *"The promises were spoken to Abraham and to his descendant. Scripture doesn't say "descendants," referring to many, but "your descendant," referring to one. That descendant is Christ. This is what I mean: The laws given to Moses 430 years after God had already put his promise to Abraham into effect didn't cancel the promise to Abraham" (Gal 3:16-17, GWT).*

In between those years, Abraham and the subsequent generations were going through these building processes outlined in this book. They were dwelling in tents (refusing to build permanent structures both physically and mentally). They were lifting holy hands and declaring the reality of their new position in God, looking for a city that has foundations in God. They refused to settle for less. They were announcing the conviction they had in their mind. They refused to be deterred by the prevailing circumstances trying to choke their human spirit in fulfilling their God-given mandate, possessing the Promised Land. They were looking for a new society, culture, lifestyle, business, relationship, profession, whose architect, designer, inventor, and Maker is God.

Another scenario displayed in Abraham's life about his declaration of his new position was when the Angel of God visited him and promised him a male child – Isaac. It took Abraham several years (about 25years) to process these principles before God fulfilled the promise.

During these periods, God changed his name from Abram to Abraham (Father of nations) and changed his wife's name from Sara to Sarah (mother of thousand). These changes occurred before God fulfilled the promise. Abraham bore the seed of Isaac in his heart for 25years without wavering at the promises of God. All he kept doing was to give glory to God and declaring his new position and status – Father of many nations as God had promised.

The Bible recorded it concerning Abraham in this wise:

> *"Who against hope believed in hope, that he might become the Father of many nations, according to that which was spoken, so shall thy seed be. And being not weak in faith, he considered not his own body now dead, when he was about a hundred years old, neither yet the deadness of Sarah's womb. He staggered not at the promise of God through unbelief; but was strong in faith, giving glory to God" (Rom 4:18-20).*

Prevailing circumstances would have prevented him, but he doused those fears and stood against nature and the evil wind arrayed against his life.

The Arrival Of The New Makes The Old Obsolete

> *"In that, He says, "A new covenant," He has made the first obsolete. Now what is becoming obsolete and growing old is ready to vanish away" (Heb 8:13).*

This scripture explains the natural order of things in life. Once a new thing comes into existence, the old begins to give way. This is what happens to an individual who had gone through these processes of building a life that is accurate before God to attract a 'thank you and well done' commendation from his Maker – the Almighty God.

The declaration of the new kick started the destruction of the old. If we don't loudly declare the new, the old will not give way. There is always a conflict between the old and the new. The old has been on the ground longer than the new and knows all the environment's nooks and crannies. The old may have more crowd (followers) than the new. With all these, the old tends to intimidate the new. But unknown to the new that what lies underneath the old is fear of loss. The old will never allow the new to declare itself openly, always suggesting many reasons why it can't work.

Engulfing darkness always seems to be in total control until an immense light appears. The appearance of light automatically dispels the engulfing darkness no matter how thick it might be. This is the same thing that happens between the old and new. This fight between the old and the new is found in all spheres of life.

This conflict between the old and the new is exemplified in King David's life. The scriptures recorded that at a time, the house of David waxed stronger and stronger while the house of Saul grew weaker and weaker. It all started with the declaration of the kingship of David by Prophet Samuel. Though the new suffer occasional attacks from the old, but it must always overcome.

> *"And the war was long between the house of Saul and the house of David; but David became continually stronger, and the house of Saul became continually weaker" (2 Samuel 3:1, Darby Translation).*

There are many suggestive words from the old designed to weaken the new. Some took place in the life of Abraham. For example: in the life of Abram announcing his new name to be Abraham, the old will ask, "What if you were wrong? What if it does not come true? People will laugh at you, and you will lose your integrity. Better wait until it comes true before you start declaring it. Instead, allow someone else to do it. Must you show yourself? There and many other suggestions as they are designed to prevent the new from manifesting.

No matter the area or field, the principles of the old is almost the same. It creates fear and intimidation to the new. The goal is to weaken the strength of its proclamation. The old understands that the declaration and emergence of the new is its demise. Therefore, the new must receive power to overcome the old's intimidation and fear and declare its existence.

The Israelite's wanderers declared that they were strangers and pilgrims on the earth (Egypt) where they were then. They said they belong to another earth (Canaan) which is like the heavenly one – the proposed earth (their own dwelling place), which has been configured into their mind by God. They had shifted their mind to it and said it was either this or nothing. They burnt the bridge of return, saying no going back.

> *"All these people died having faith. They didn't receive the things that God had promised them, but they saw these things coming in the distant future and rejoiced. They acknowledged that they were living as strangers with no permanent home on earth. 14 Those who say such things make it clear that they are looking for their own country. 15 If they had been thinking about the country that they had left, they could have found a way to go back. 16 Instead, these men were longing for a better country—a heavenly country. That is why God is not ashamed to be called their God. He has prepared a city for them" (Heb 11:13-16, GWT).*

God wants us to forge ahead in the new things He is doing in our lives despite the increasing darkness all around us. We have to speak and allow God to make it good at His own time, despite the satanic assault against our advancement and the fear of whether it will come to pass or not. We have to resist the words of men trying to evaluate us by their standards. Though the giants from the children of Anakim were in Jericho, Joshua and Caleb declared God's word amidst the formidable opposition against them. It was in their declaration that their strength and salvation came.

Part of this declaration is the physical repositioning of ourselves in what we have heard from the Lord. This repositioning has to do with strategic planning and physical dislocation into the new environment. In preparing for the word of the Lord, we must accurately position ourselves where the word will meet us. As a man, if the Lord reveals that you will bear children, you must get yourself a wife in preparation for that word to come to pass. If you are to become an academician or a lecturer, you must study to obtain at least a Master's degree.

We must come to a place of competence and skill acquisition under a more versed mentor in whatever field God is calling us into. Imagine a man who keeps declaring that God wants him to be a university lecturer to affect lives but refuses to study the requisite courses. If he likes, he should pray and fast for the rest of his life; it can't happen. Until he migrates to a physical position, he can never achieve that purpose. Without the personal choice and commitment to act on what God has said about your life, it can't come to pass. It will remain an illusion.

The New Jerusalem (the new earth) coming down from heaven will occur through the decrees and declarations of faithful and true saints. Their collective pronouncements of the will of God on the earth will bring it to pass in the same frequency at which it was spoken in heaven. This is a significant demand that would bring the Kingdom of heaven to earth.

God is restoring the Apostolic grace in this season to declare what God has said concerning planet earth. This declaration is coming with enormous strength and power to enforce God's will on earth. It is not just prayers but executive anointing to bring to be what is not yet in place. God's declaration created the first heaven and earth. The Prophetic and Apostolic saints' declaration will create the new heaven and the new earth. These Prophetic and Apostolic saints are representations of the mouth and the Lord's hand, respectively. Hey saints! Wake up to this glorious and clarion call.

> *"And you forget the Lord your Maker, Who stretched out the heavens And laid the foundations of the earth; You have feared continually every day Because of the fury of the oppressor When he has prepared to destroy. And where is the fury of the oppressor?"*
>
> *I have covered you with the shadow of My hand, That I may [a]plant the heavens, Lay the foundations of the earth, And say to Zion, 'You are My people" (Isa. 51:13, 16, NKJV).*

Verse 13 of this scripture is about the creation of the first heaven and earth. It was done by the Godhead alone. There was no collaboration with man in that creation.

Verse 16 is different from verse 13. The creation of the new heaven and the new earth will be in collaboration with man. The Godhead is going to work together with the part of the body of Christ called the mouth and the hand which is represented by the prophetic and the apostolic saints, respectively, in building the new heaven and the new earth. This will take the form of mighty declarations of what God has said concerning the earth.

A CALL FOR PRAYER

- *Ask the Lord to strengthen your inner man and fortify you by the anointing of the Holy Ghost to execute His counsel in your life without fear or favor.*

- *Ask the Lord to embolden you to announce Him and His doings in the earth in the area and capacity He has given you.*

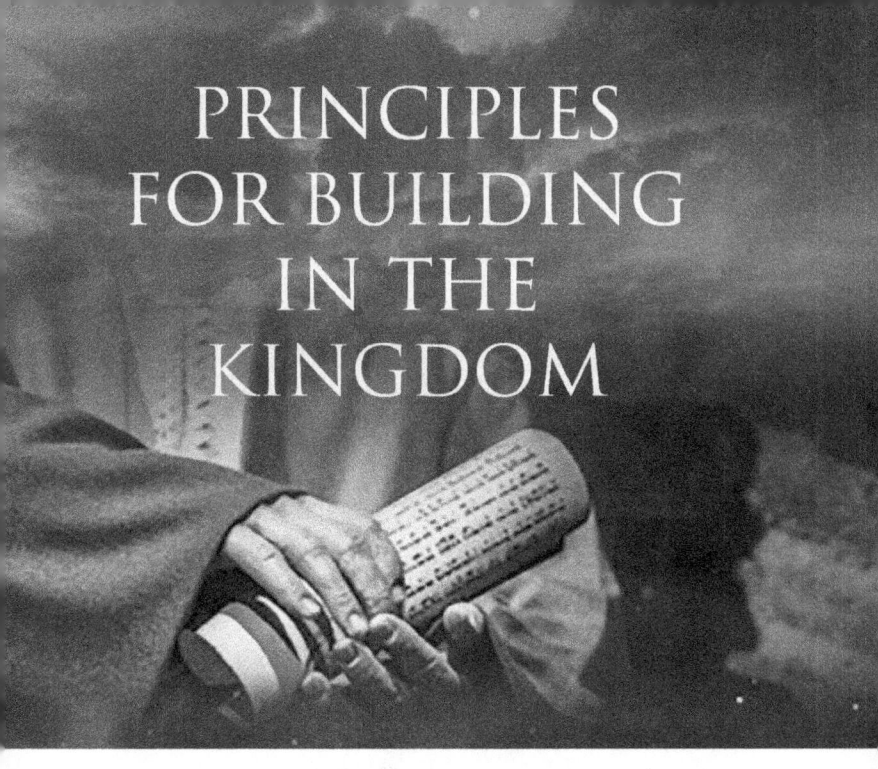

PRINCIPLES FOR BUILDING IN THE KINGDOM

CHAPTER 6

Hindrances To This Building

As good as building a life plan, eternal structures, and careers that will receive God's approval and stand the test of time is, some factors could limit this building from rising to the most significant height God has ordained for it.

We need to deal with specific values, lifestyles, mentalities, and belief systems both from within and outside us to build accurately. The book of Hebrews 12:1 calls these limitations, weight, and sin that easily ensnares us. They limit us from accomplishing our God-given goals. They do not allow us to advance. They make us complacent with our condition. They turn us away from God's plans and divert our attention to our selfish pursuits. This weight and sin stagnate and eventually destroys us spiritually. We may still be born-again, but certainly, we will not be able to reach the maximum height God has planned for us on earth.

The kingdom of God is an advancing kingdom, and only <u>forceful men</u> can discern its frequency of operation. Anything that resists our force of advance to this building is a hindrance. To advance means to move forward, but in a particular direction (towards God's direction and nothing more). The **Bible** says, *"Woe to him who is at ease in Zion."* You can be at ease in two ways: the first, you can be where you are and refuse to move towards the direction of God. The second is that you might be moving but no longer in the direction God has planned for you. In the eyes of God, the day you stop moving towards Him is the day you stop moving, even though you might be building but for yourself or Babylon. No matter what you have achieved for God, there is always the next level in Him.

INTERNAL HINDRANCE TO THE BUILDING

Inaccurate hegemony of the mind: Phil 3:3-9

"For we are the circumcisions who worship God in the spirit, rejoice in Christ Jesus, and have no confidence in the

flesh, though I also might have confidence in the flesh. If anyone else thinks he may have confidence in the flesh, I more so: circumcised the eight-day, of the stock of Israel, of the tribe of Benjamin a Hebrew of the Hebrews; concerning the law, a Pharisee; concerning zeal, persecuting the church; concerning the righteousness which is in the law, blameless. But what things were gain to me, <u>these I have counted loss for Christ.</u> Yet indeed I also count all things loss for the excellence of the knowledge of Christ Jesus my Lord, for whom I have suffered the loss of all things, and counted them as rubbish, that I may gain Christ and be found in Him, not having my own righteousness, which is from the law but that which is through faith in Christ, the righteousness which is from God by faith."

Paul recounted all the values and criteria (qualifications) that motivated most of his actions before his transformation. He had enough reason to boast of what he had achieved in God as most of us will do today when the occasion presents itself. However, Paul regretted and discarded everything he did in that scripture, counting them as a loss to gain Christ. He made a 'U' turn in his journey.

Paul reconstructed the forefront of his mind. He built a new philosophy within his mind to the degree that the things of God instinctively became more valuable to him. In contrast, the things of the earth he had always boasted of instinctively became worthless. We ought always to take this posture whenever we face issues demanding to call up our self-worth.

Hegemony in this context, means things we value most that take precedence or priority over others. These are things that take place in us without our conscious thinking when the occasion demands. It is the first filter of the mind through which everything else passes. It determines how we view and interpret everything, whether it is God or anything else.

The hegemony of your mind determines what and how you build. Indeed, you may be building, but are you building with the specification given by God? Paul's earthly qualifications defined his original hegemony.

Let us closely examine some examples of Paul's inaccurate hegemony in Philippians Chapter 3 as a metric to examine our hegemony. The first erroneous hegemony in Paul's life was his strong confidence in his accomplishments. He had enough reasons to boast of his qualifications. He had degrees that could easily attract attention from anyone. He was an erudite scholar in his days. He came from an ideal home, well brought up, highly disciplined, respects everybody around, attends church services constantly and loves the things of God, and is modest in the real sense of it. These are credentials worth boasting, which Paul believed he had more than most of his contemporaries. He was the only scholar among the Apostles. It is worthy of note to say that Paul was already a believer before experiencing this transformation. Most of us behave like Paul.

He got the sense of value, worth, and identity from being of the tribe of Benjamin, "Hebrew of the Hebrews, and the son of Abraham. He was building his life according to the world's principles which will not allow him to build according to God's principles.

He also had an ego, which is another system of definition that shapes our worldview. It tells us who we are. Paul allowed his natural-based values such as his status, education, background, and achievements to define him instead of God, from where he originally came.

He needed a mental shift to view this building the way God wanted him to view it. During Paul's life transformation in Phil 3:3-9, he undertook specific actions to bring the necessary changes. These points would help us make changes as we embark on our journey in our building process.

They are as follows:-

The Calculation Of Loss: He counted all that he valued most as if they never existed. The issue here is not that achievements are wrong but your source of inspiration. Is it God, you, or your environment? He counted as dung all that he got by himself and the environment.

Redefinition Of His Starting Context: He now realized that his starting point in life is Christ and not his earthly lineage. He knew that he had been in existence before the world began and would continue till eternity. He has been in God all the while and came into existence by the breath of God. He realized that God named him, not his parent, the society, his achievements, or the world's philosophy. He has to function by the rhythm of God's music.

Conforming To The Death Of Christ: In this building process, the only edifice that will last the test of time and receive God's final approval are the ones built on the knowledge and the power of the Lord. This will happen based on our conformity to His suffering and His death. We can only see His works in our lives and build on them in proportion to our death to self and the vices of the world.

Ability To Strain Heavenwards: This is not about going to heaven but a craving to be in His likeness and make His preference our preference. Take a look at Colossians 3:1-3 in NLT and AMP versions.

> *"Since you have been raised to new life with Christ, set your sights on the realities of heaven, not the things of the earth. For you died to his life, and your real life is hidden with Christ in God" (NLT).*

> *"If then you have been raised with Christ to a new life, thus sharing his resurrection from the dead, aim at and seek the rich, eternal treasures that are above, where Christ is,*

seated at the right hand of God. And set your minds and keep them set on what is above (the higher things), not on the thing that are on the earth. For as far as this world is concerned, you have died, and your new, real life is hidden with Christ in God" (AMP).

Straining heavenwards means living a life with higher values, changed mentalities, living above the world's standards, and being governed by the laws of God from the inside engraved in our hearts, as opposed to the laws on the two tablets of stone.

External Hindrances To The Building

Lack Of Focus: This is a significant obstacle to building whatever will last the test of time in the sight of God. See what Paul, the wise master builder says in Phil 3:13;

"Brethren, I do not count myself to have apprehended; but this one thing I do, forgetting those things which are behind and reaching forward to those things which are ahead."

The emphasis here is **"one thing I do."** Lack of focus and consistency can rob us of the plan of God for our lives. On our journey in building what is accurate in God's sight, several obstacles intend to swerve our hearts away from the purpose of God, but with focus and resilience, we will remain on track. Concentrated focus is the antidote to the enemy's distraction. The Bible recorded that Jesus endured the cross and despised the shame (obstacles and hindrances) because of the joy set before him to become the Lord of all lords and King of all kings. He kept on gazing at the purpose and pushing forward. Our continuous gazing at the purpose with sustained momentum will frustrate the enemies of our building. James says a double-minded man is unstable in all his ways. He says let him not ever think he will receive anything from the Lord. Lack of focus breeds instability.

Competition And Rivalry: God created every human to be unique in all things. We can learn some attitudes from one another, but the real you who make up your destiny is unique. The day we begin to copy or compete with others in terms of our destiny, we reduce ourselves to a second-class person both in the eyes of God and people. We can never see what God is saying about us to build on it.

Competition will always lead to rivalry and war. The Bible says, **"*He that compares himself with people is not wise.*"** We desire to be like someone else or even get what they have. We believe that if something is working in someone's life, it must work in my life without knowing if that is what God ordained for me or not.

Take a look at this scripture in James 4:1-3;

"What is causing the quarrels and fight among you? Isn't it because there is a whole army of evil desires within you?

> *You want what you don't have, so you kill to have it. You long for what others have, and you can't afford it, so you start a fight to take it away from them. And yet, the reason you don't have is that you don't ask God for it. And even when you do ask, you don't get it because your whole aim is wrong- you want only what will give you pleasure."*

We fight so much in churches where believers are because of wrong desires. We even form a song as a result; *"If God must bless someone, it must be me."*

Presumptuous Activities: To be presumptuous in building that which will receive God's approval is a risk we must avoid at all cost. Most times, believers make several assumptions about God. Presumptuous sin is a great offense. It attracts the same consequences as one who never did anything. To presume means to suppose that something is correct, although we do not have the actual proof, to accept something as accurate without analyzing whether it is real or not.

David, at a time in his life, sinned presumptuously and paid dearly for it. He decided to bring the Ark of the Lord to his house. This was not wrong, but instead of asking the proper way to carry the Ark, he devised his own method and chose to carry it on a new cart.

> *"So they carried the ark of God from the house of Abinadab on a new cart, with Uzzah and Ahio guiding the cart"* (1 Chr 13:7, BSB).

David presumed that having the Ark on a brand new cart would be more profound and dignified both to him as a king and even to God than mere humans carrying it on their shoulders as prescribed by God.

> "And the Levites carried the ark of God on their shoulders with the poles, as Moses had commanded in accordance with the word of the LORD" (1 Chronicle15:15, BSB).

A brand new cart is likened to the latest brand new car in our today's world. The King presumed that carrying the Ark of the Lord would have been done in a way to show greatness and glory. He wanted to show his love to God, his passion, and his readiness to give his best for God. Unfortunately, he never realized that the action would cost someone's life and truncate God's purpose. It was as serious as that.

> "When they came to the threshing floor of Chidond Uzzah reached out and took hold of the Ark because the oxen had stumbled. And the anger of the LORD burned against Uzzah, and He struck him down because he had put his hand on the Ark. So he died there before God" (1chr 13:7, BSB).

To have the desire to do well is no longer enough. We must go beyond the desires to knowing how to do it in God's way so that God can say to us, "well done, my good and faithful servants." To be a philanthropist is good but may or may not attract God's attention and approval anymore.

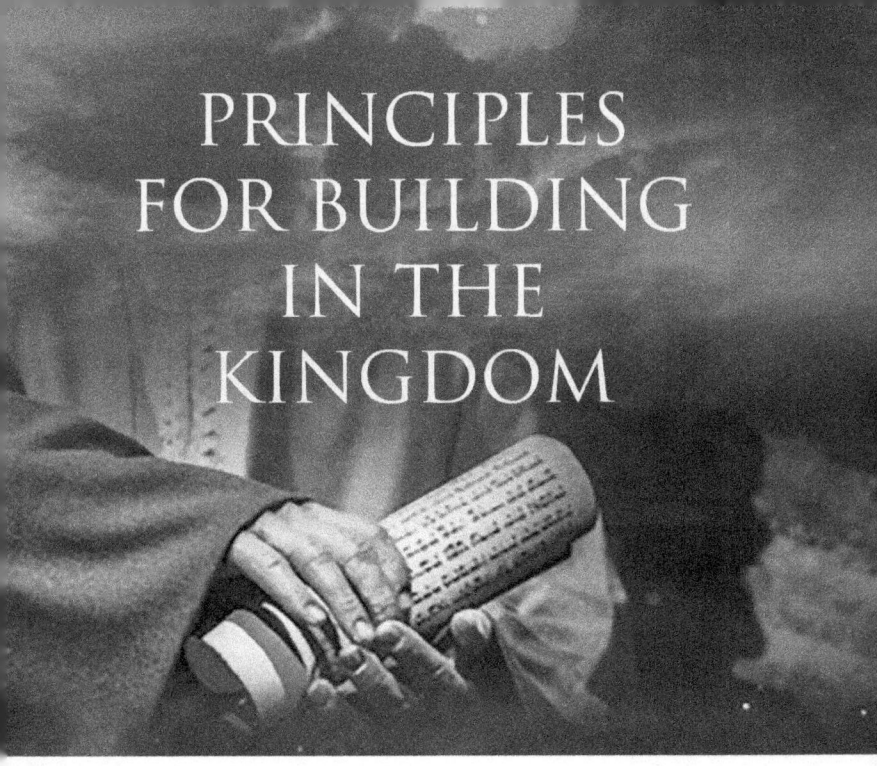

PRINCIPLES FOR BUILDING IN THE KINGDOM

CHAPTER 7

An Awakening To Build

"Then I answered them, and said to them, The God of heaven himself will prosper us, therefore we his servants will arise and build, but you have no heritage or right or memorial in Jerusalem" (Neh 2:20).

"So the Lord stirred up the spirit of Zerubbabel the son of Shealtiel, the governor of Judah, and the spirit of Joshua the son of Jehozadak, the high priest and the spirit of all

the remnant of the people and they came and worked on the house of the Lord of hosts, their God" (Haggai 1:14).

"Who are you, o great mountain before Zerubbabel? You shall become a plain! And he shall bring forth the capstone with shouts of 'Grace, Grace to it. The hands of Zerubbabel have laid the foundation of this temple; his hands shall also finish it. Then you shall know that the Lord of hosts had sent me to you"(Zech 4:7, 9).

God is putting His Spirit upon believers to build according to His pattern and design. We are in the days of building, and we must build. The spirit of the wise master builder is being deposited in believers' lives these days of the last hour. We are to build in these days of increasing darkness in the nations of the earth when the hearts of men are failing them. We are to build in these last days when the word of God is scarce, and people are running to and fro, from pillar to post, searching for the true word of God. We are to build in these days of reproach when 'seven women' are thronging to one man not to eat his food or ask for anything but to remove reproach from them. We are to massively build in these last days when crises are taking over the nations of the earth, and everyone is looking for help. The real help comes from Zion.

God is charging those who fear Him to stretch forth their faith in boldness and build without intimidation in the face of resistance and opposition.

We are to build, just like in Noah's days when he spoke differently from what the rest of the world were saying for the space of 120 years.

We should build like in the days of Job's when he focused his heart on God, while others concentrate on self and their environment.

We should build like in the days of Enoch, who prophesied about the Lord's coming to judge those who never cared about God or His words.

We should build like in the days of Nehemiah, who singlehandedly opposed and confronted the occult warlords of his days, withstanding them to their feet, not minding their harassments and threats to weaken the work of God in his hands.

We should build like in Deborah's days when no male was ready to lead in the battle of the Lord against the mighty (Judges5:23).

We should build like in the days of Phinehas who turned away God's wrought through his zealousness for God in wiping away corruption out of Israel (Num25:7-13).

The list continues. The story will not be complete if your name is not mentioned. These people fought on behalf of our King (Jesus) and His Kingdom; they resisted the powers of darkness in their time, stood for righteousness, and displayed the nature and lifestyle of the heavenly Kingdom here on earth. The baton is being handed over to us now. Can we represent heaven's interest amid confusing and conflicting interests within our environment? Can God count on us to deliver our environment to Him? The Spirit of the Lord spoke passionately through Isaiah His prophet in two places for the sake of emphasis, saying:

> *"Awake, awake, put on strength, o arm of the Lord, awake as in the ancient days, in the generations of old. Art thou not it which hath dried the sea, the water of the great deep, that hath made the depths of the sea a way for the ransomed to pass over" (Isa51:9-10)?*

> *"Awake, awake put on thy strength, O Zion, put on thy beautiful garments, o Jerusalem, the holy city, for henceforth, there shall no more come into thee the uncircumcised and the uncleaned, shake thyself from the dirt, arise and sit down, o Jerusalem. Loose thyself from the band of thy neck, o captive daughter of Zion" (Isa52:1-2).*

There is a demand to arise with strength at this hour. There is a negotiation over the soul of the nations of the earth. God is looking up to us to wake up and put on our strength for the battle ahead. This is the battle of the mighty. The fathers of old have done great works, but we are to complete the work as it was written.

> *"And all these, having obtained a good testimony through faith, did not receive the promise, God having provided something better for us, that they should not be made perfect apart from us"* (Heb 11:39-40).

Building The New Heaven And The New Earth

> *"And I saw a new heaven and a new earth, for the first heaven and first earth had passed away, and there was no more sea. And I John saw the holy city, a New Jerusalem, coming down from God out of heaven, prepared as a bride adorned for her husband. And I heard a great voice out of heaven saying, Behold the tabernacle of God is with men, and He will dwell with them, and they shall be his people, and God himself shall be with them and be their God"* (Rev 21:1-3).

In this scripture, a new heaven and new earth are coming. There will not be any again (no more boundaries between heaven and the earth. The New Jerusalem is coming from God through the word out of heaven. This heaven refers to our spirit man. As the saints of the end time engage in warfare by declaring God's intent, aligning their lifestyles with the current speaking of God, and living righteously, the principles and foundations of Babylon would be destroyed, and the new heaven and new earth will emerge.

Revisit these scriptures:

> *"And I have put my words in your mouth, I have covered you with the shadows of my hand that I may plant the heavens, lay the foundations of the earth, and say to Zion 'you are my people"* (Isa51:16).

> *"And you forget the Lord your Maker, who stretched out the heavens and laid the foundation of the earth" (Isa51:3a).*

In the first scripture, the building of heaven and the earth is in the past tense, indicating that it was done by God alone. The building is in the future tense in the second scripture, suggesting it is not done yet. Again, it is not just God alone that will do it but with the collaboration of the apostolic and prophetic saints (mouth-(to speak), which refers to the prophetic while (hand-(to do or act) which refers to the apostolic).

The Lord is raising an army equipped with the prophetic and apostolic spirit to make declarations in the nations of the earth. These declarations are not about success or prosperity but structures and systems of God's governance on earth. The declaration is like this: thy will be done on earth in the same frequency in heaven. Let thy Kingdom be established on planet earth as water covers the sea.

Not every church member will partake in this unfolding event but the remnant that the Lord will choose. Are you part of this remnant? You can be enlisted in this group if you position yourself. In what area within your capacity are you preparing for this awesome event? There is a clarion call for the 'Joshua Generation' who will fight on behalf of God over a territory. A people whose allegiance is only to God and His Kingdom, they cared not about their own lives neither the lives of their loved ones.

In this dispensation, there will be seamless interaction between heaven and the earth. It will be as it was in Adam's days at the cool of the day when God could come to interact with Adam. Saints could transverse the two realms easily without any limitation. No more sea means no more demarcation or obstruction or hindrance to reaching the two realms.

The Opposer Of The Finish

God intends that a generation will accomplish all His words, thereby closing this Church age. With the finishing grace, this generation will bring to fulfillment all the written prophesies in the scriptures. They will point the Church to the end. The Church's dispensation has a beginning and also an end. God is looking up to a generation that will stand out to end it when all things would have been gathered unto God by Christ Jesus. God is raising a vast majority of believers to do this. He equips them with all required to break the seal of God's word, mature them into His likeness, and perform His will on earth. He is raising a new species of humans whose DNA is God, whose origin does not proceed from the earth, and they don't derive their identity from their surroundings. We call them "The Ultimate Generation."

As God is raising these groups of people on earth, the devil who opposes this finishing grace is also strategizing to ensure the Church does not finish well. He wants to ensure that the Church does not grow to maturity, thereby knowing her full rights and privileges concerning God's plan for her on earth.

The devil's greatest undoing is the Church maximizing capacity to fulfill God's purposes on earth. He resists the Church from getting to this finishing line by not allowing her to build accurately according to the pattern God has set for her. He can allow the Church to have money, power, influence, and anything she wants, but he keeps her distracted from God's purpose. He is committed not to let the Church grow to maturity in God but shall always fail. He does this through several means, which are the following:

The Opposer's Strategies To Prevent The Church From Getting To The Finish Line

Misplaced Priorities: The opposer places different agendas for the Church to pursue, distracting her from seeing the essence of why she is here on earth. On the mount of transfiguration, God revealed some realities about His plans for global redemption, but Peter was busy thinking about building tabernacles for Jesus, Moses, and Elijah. Again Peter tried to prevent Jesus from dying when the opportunity came for Jesus to liberate the world through His death on the cross as the sacrificial Lamb of God.

Lack Of Unity Among Brethren: The opposer creates disunity among believers, so they don't come together to fulfill their God-given purpose. It will take kings (a group of matured believers) to search out the hidden treasures of God. No single saint will be able to do it.

> *"It is the glory of God to conceal a matter; to search out a matter is the glory of kings" (Prov. 25:2, NIV).*

Inability To Seek The Deeper Things Of God: The Church refusing to grow into sonship (adulthood) has prevented her from entering into the full plan of God. To continue to be children will never give us our inheritance, and hence we cannot finish well.

> *"Now I say that the heir, as long as he is a child, does not differ at all from a slave, though he is master of all, but is under guardians and stewards until the time appointed by the father" (Galatians 4:-2).*

A False Religious Desire For God: The opposer creates a false desire for God, depriving people of seeing the reality and accuracy of God's true nature and His dealings on earth. This is just a form of godliness devoid of the power of God.

A Desire For God's Gifts And Not The Giver: The opposer is ready to allow the Church to acquire gifts such as miracles, power, success, and the like without desiring the Giver of the gifts. To them, the acquisition of wealth is equal to godliness. Without the formation of Christ-likeness in the life of believers, we can never get to the finish.

Materialism And Cares Of This World: The opposer creates activities, professionalism, and economy dedicated to work instead of dedication to God. Godliness has become old-fashioned that cannot be practiced in our today's world. Globalization and technology now run the world, no longer God or His principles.

A Desire For Comfort And Complacency: The opposer places self-need (desire to achieve the best of life) in place of heaven's need over our life. He creates a craving for ease, relaxation, enjoyment, and care for the body more than caring for the spirit. These words are ultimately not in line with the scriptures. We will never get to the finish with those words.

Lack Of Prophetic Sight: The opposer seeks every means to ensure the Church does not comprehend the depth of God's eternal plan for her. He is responsible for the partial blindness of the Church.

Lack Of Strong Faith To Execute The Purposes Of God: The opposer makes it difficult for the Church to climb the mountain of higher faith in God. He puts some hurdles on their way. He shows them human success rather than divine achievements.

CLOSING PRAYER

- *Lord Jesus Christ, you are the builder of all things. Grant us the sight, the ear, and the heart to build according to your divine intent.*

- *Lord, let our lives match with your purpose and intent on this planet earth.*

- *Lord, let us become the change agents and tools in your hand to bring the necessary change you desire to see on this planet earth.*

- *Lord grant us our heart's desire in Jesus' name we pray. Amen.*

Other Book Authored By
TONY AZONUCHE

Tony is a skillful and a prolific writer, and a business strategist with vast experience in the subject matters of the Gospel of the Kingdom and the King and His Kingdom. He is a Dynamic

Minister of the Lord Jesus Christ, with an unflinching passion to see the full manifestation of the Kingdom of God here on earth.

Tony is the Convener of the Joshua Generation Movement, a Kingdom-based organization poised to execute the mandate of God: *"Thy kingdom come, thy will be done on earth as it is done in heaven.*

THE PURPOSE OF THE CHURCH ON EARTH

In this book, the author has lucidly revealed the significance and urgency of why every believer must understand the purpose of the Church on earth. The Lord Jesus made an unequivocal statement at the declaration of His Church that the gates of hell shall not prevail against her. Ever since, there has been a relentless opposition against the Church and its purpose on earth; therefore, it is our responsibility as believers to enforce the commands of the Lord Jesus Christ.

The book explains the different components of the Church and what to do to enforce God's Kingdom on earth before the return of Jesus amidst the Babylonian principles that govern the world in opposition to God's Kingdom principles.

Find out those Kingdom principles and how to apply them to your daily life, and influence your world for Jesus.

Get copies for yourself, friends and families.

It is a must read for every Kingdom-minded believer.

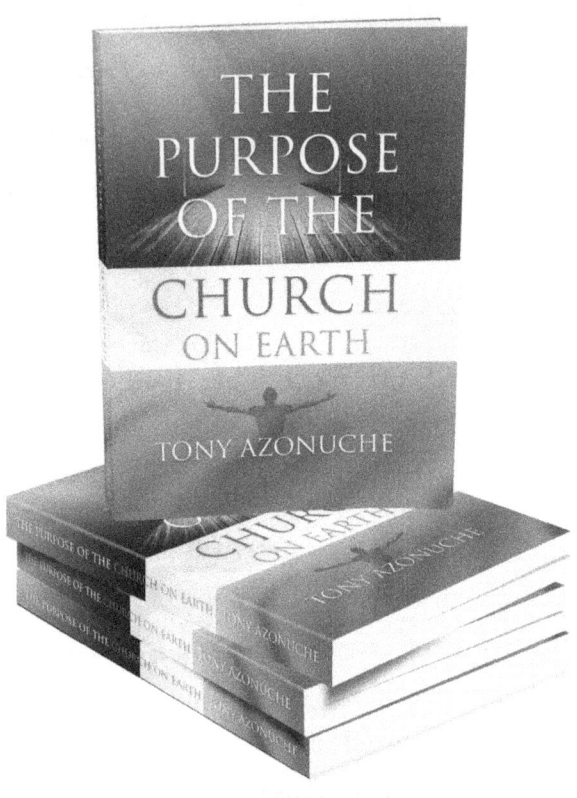

HOW TO GET COPIES OF HIS BOOKS

You can order copies Online on www.amazon.com

OR

Author's Direct Contact
Tony Azonuche
tonyazonuche@gmail.com
Tel: 1 (832) 419-7961, (832) 419-7988
Convener: Joshua Generation Movement.
joshuagenmovt@gmail.com
For Teachings, Seminars, Workshops on Kingdom Dimensions.

Reflection Point

Personal Notes:

Guided Action Plan

Reflection Point

Personal Notes:

Guided Action Plan

Reflection Point

Personal Notes:

===== *Guided Action Plan* =====

Reflection Point

Personal Notes:

Guided Action Plan

www.ingramcontent.com/pod-product-compliance
Lightning Source LLC
Chambersburg PA
CBHW051652040426
42446CB00009B/1104